Emily Dickinson

MILTON MELTZER

Emily Dickinson

A BIOGRAPHY

Twenty-First Century Books
Minneapolis

Also by Milton Meltzer

Herman Melville: A Biography

Edgar Allan Poe: A Biography

Walt Whitman: A Biography

Carl Sandburg: A Biography

Langston Hughes

Dorothea Lange: A Photographer's Life

Lincoln in His Own Words

Frederick Douglass in His Own Words

Ten Queens: Portraits of Women of Power

Ten Kings and the Worlds They Ruled

There Comes a Time: The Struggle for Civil Rights

They Came in Chains: The Story of the Slave Ships

Witches and Witch Hunts: A History of Persecution

The Day the Sky Fell: A History of Terrorism

The Cotton Gin

The Printing Press

Contents

   ~   Foreword   9

1 ~   Shout for Joy   11

2 ~   Lessons for Humanity   16

3 ~   I Shall Keep Singing   21

4 ~   Opening Her Eyes   27

5 ~   Study, Work, and Meditate   32

6 ~   A Bequest of Wings   41

7 ~   Valentine's Day   53

8 ~   A Trip "Abroad"   58

9 ~   Independent as the Sun   65

10 ~   A Choice Spirit   71

11 ~   My Business Is to Love   80

12 ~   I Find Ecstasy in Living   88

13 ∿ You Are a Great Poet   96

14 ∿ O My Too Beloved   101

15 ∿ They'll Have to Remember Me   108

16 ∿ In Print, At Last   114

∿ Source Notes   117

∿ Selected Bibliography   119

∿ Chronology of Emily Dickinson's Life   121

∿ Visiting the Emily Dickinson sites   124

∿ Index   125

∿ About the Author   128

Foreword

Words, words, words . . .

Everybody has them. Everybody uses them. They are what brings us all together, and what makes us all different.

For poets, words are life's blood. In every culture, poets sing, sing for the sheer love of it. Their poems may shout for joy or weep for loss. They may be short or long, complex or simple. Some are intimate, a personal confession. The way some poets use words may not make for easy reading. But what comes easy is often not worth very much.

Emily Dickinson, born in Amherst, Massachusetts, in 1830, died in that small town in 1886. Very few people beyond her neighborhood heard about her during her lifetime. Only a handful of her poems had reached print, and not by her doing. Yet she astonished the world a few years after her death when volumes of her poetry began to be published. More than 1,700 poems had been written on scraps of paper in the quiet of her room, found there in little packets by her sister. The best of them, said one critic, are as international as sunshine. Proof of their outreach to all humanity is seen in the fact that her work has been published in dozens of languages.

How did Emily Dickinson come to create poetry that has won her acclaim as one of the greatest writers in the English language?

What factors in her upbringing, her schooling, and the culture of that time combined to make words her refuge and her great love?

Watching a little bird in her garden, she said, "Wherefore sing, since nobody hears?"

Let's try to find out why she sang.

1

Shout for Joy

WHAT WAS IT LIKE to be born a Dickinson in the town of Amherst? Well, it was not like being born a princess in a royal family. But it was special, nevertheless. The infant Emily first saw the light of day on December 10, 1830. She was luckier than most newborns of her time—for several reasons. First: she survived. And so did her mother. Women ran a great risk of dying in childbirth. And only one out of eight babies lived into his or her second year.

Emily's ancestry too gave her an advantage. Dickinsons were among the earliest settlers in America. They arrived from England in the 1630s and settled in Massachusetts, with farming their way of earning a living. Like other white immigrants, they fought to push the "heathen" Indians out of their homelands. Later, Dickinsons took part in the French and Indian War and soldiered in George Washington's Revolutionary army.

Those first New England Puritans meant to establish in this wilderness "a New Jerusalem, a city upon a hill, to the glory of God." Dickinsons would become ministers, legislators, judges, generals, governors. Their toughness and independence were traits Emily too would possess. Amherst alone had five Congregational churches, all of them religiously conservative.

When Emily was born, the American nation was only some fifty-five years old. It was still a land of farms and small towns. In 1830 the population was 13 million. Today Pennsylvania alone has just as many people. Only one of every fifteen citizens lived in cities of over eight thousand.

Emily would never move away from her birthplace. Nestled in a valley plateau, Amherst was circled by forested hills. It was one of the loveliest landscapes in New England, whose changing seasons Emily always gloried in.

Amherst held about three thousand people. It was named for Lord Jeffrey Amherst, the British general in the French and Indian War who recommended the use of smallpox-infected blankets to wipe out the Indians. While other towns in the region would grow during Emily's time, Amherst changed but little. It was hardly touched by the spirit of business enterprise that had seized America right after the American Revolution. For several decades now, factories had been opening, many of them in New England, a few in Amherst. Cotton and woolen mills were dominant. By the early 1800s half the nation's textile workers were under ten years of age, working twelve or more hours a day.

Most people didn't think there was anything wrong with this. There was a universal belief in the goodness of work, and a strong fear of idleness. A popular saying of the time was, "The devil will find things for idle hands to do."

The typical American expected to become a capitalist and rich. For any hardworking, ambitious person, enterprise was a kind of religion. Emily's grandfather and father chose a professional path, the practice of law. They strove to be leaders in their field and to accumulate fortunes that would guarantee the comfort and security of their families.

The Amherst, Massachusetts of Emily's childhood was hardly the bustling college town that it is today. In the middle distance on the left side of the street, you can see the gabled Dickinson Homestead.

Emily's paternal grandfather, Samuel Fowler Dickinson, became one of the region's foremost lawyers. Ambitious and public spirited, he served many terms in the Massachusetts legislature.

The Amherst folk praised Samuel as "a ferocious worker and a born leader, a man of ideas and principles." He was a founder of both Amherst Academy and Amherst College. The academy was a private classical school, giving instruction in the humanities, the fine arts, and the broad aspects of science. The college

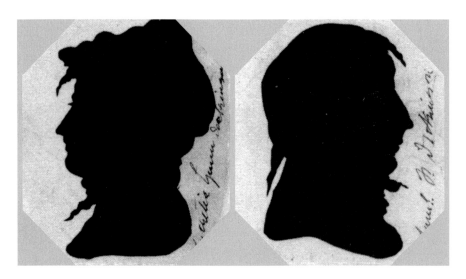

Samuel Fowler Dickinson and his wife, Lucretia Gunn, are shown here in cut-paper silhouettes, a fashionable art form of their time. Edward, Emily's father, born in 1803, was the eldest of their nine children.

had an initial enrollment of forty-seven students, with two teachers and the president. Its stated goal was the education of "promising but needy youths who wished to enter the ministry."

Not only was Emily's grandfather a bulwark of the new college but so were her father and her brother. These two would serve in turn as the college's treasurer for a total of some sixty years. Unlike most men of the time, Samuel publicly supported the education of women. Daughters, he said, should be "well instructed" in the arts and sciences. "The female mind so sensitive . . . should not be neglected. God hath designed nothing in vain."

But in the long struggle to set Amherst College on a sound footing, Samuel sacrificed both his health and his law practice, slipping close to bankruptcy. In the end, he had to leave town for a job in the Midwest, where he soon died, "disillusioned, neglected, and forgotten."

While Emily's grandfather made no mark in literature, he did display talent as a public speaker and essayist. At his graduation, Dartmouth College chose Samuel to give a major address. He dealt with the nature of government and its influence on society. Two years later he gave the patriotic oration for a Fourth of July celebration. He closed with the wish that all the world might enjoy America's freedom: "Then shall the morning Stars again, sing together, and all the sons of men shout for joy."

Samuel and his wife, Lucretia Gunn, had nine children. By the time the fifth was born, he felt the family needed more living space. He wanted a handsome home that would suit his standing as an eminent citizen. He built Amherst's first brick house, the Dickinson Homestead.

Here Emily would be born.

2

Lessons for Humanity

EMILY'S FATHER, EDWARD DICKINSON, was Samuel's oldest child. At about twelve, he began to study at the new Amherst Academy. Although religious training came first, courses in the sciences and foreign languages were important too.

At sixteen, Edward entered Yale College and proved to be a superb student, graduating in 1823. Ambitious to advance, he wanted to move to Boston to study in a law office there. Samuel wouldn't hear of his son leaving Amherst. But, as his grip on the family loosened, the four younger sons would escape to make their living in other parts of the country.

As for Edward, he stayed to read law in his father's office, eventually becoming his partner. When he was twenty-five, Edward married Emily Norcross, twenty-three, after a two-year courtship, mostly by letters. Their correspondence shows little sign of delight or passion in their relationship. They sounded more like friends than lovers. Living on her family's farm not far off, she visited the Dickinson family only once. They married in

Edward Dickinson, Emily's father, had a strong interest in literature that apparently was not shared by his wife.

a private ceremony in 1828. It was soon clear that her life would be confined to caring for home and children, while his would be devoted to the business of law and to public service.

While Edward was an avid reader, his wife showed little interest in literature. It didn't bother him, for he wanted no "literary female" at the head of his household. It was his job to do the family's thinking and talking. And so far as we know, Mrs. Dickinson was obedient and quiet.

On April 16, 1829, the young couple had their first child, a boy. They named him Austin, after one of the three brothers Mrs.

The Dickinson family homestead, built by grandfather Samuel Fowler Dickinson, and the home of Emily's parents when she was born.

Dickinson had lost to tuberculosis. In 1830, when she was pregnant with their second child, Edward bought from his father the western half of the brick house on Main Street. While the son's income was rising, the father's was falling. Inevitably this joint occupancy would lead to "border disputes" between the two generations. It was not a happy birthplace for the new baby—a girl, the Emily Dickinson who would grow into the poet.

In 1833 the couple had their third and last child, Lavinia. That they had no more was probably due to Mrs. Dickinson's uncertain health. As the two girls grew older, they sometimes had to take over the household work as well as nursing their mother.

Those were tiring duties, and boring, but the girls don't seem to have resented them.

Then too they admired their mother for her sharing of "the joys and calamities" among the families of Amherst, rich and poor. She often visited among the neighbors, offering fruit and flowers to newcomers as well as to friends. She volunteered for community and church service and at county fairs won prizes for both her cooking and her garden produce.

Emily Norcross Dickinson passed along to her daughter considerable domestic skill. After marrying Edward, she was known to frequently consult The Frugal Housewife *by Lydia Maria Child, a popular handbook of housekeeping, containing recipes, instruction in economy, and moral advice for raising children.*

Except for those times when her strength failed her, Mrs. Dickinson did all she could for her family. She was an excellent housekeeper and, as a friend put it, "a rare and delicate cook," skills she taught Emily. Her talent for gardening Emily acquired early on, creating an herbarium of her own. As her biographer Richard B. Sewall wrote, Emily learned from her mother "what was perhaps more valuable than anything a brilliant mother could have given her: lessons in simple, devoted humanity. . . ."

Because of Edward's growing prominence as a successful lawyer, the Dickinsons were often host to distinguished visitors. They would come to Amherst for events at the college or to lecture at the lyceum. At such times, as we shall see, Emily touched at least the fringes of the outside world.

A far more frequent link to events of national significance was provided by the press. The family read local and regional newspapers and such major magazines as *Harper's* and the *Atlantic Monthly*. What she absorbed from family life was influenced, of course, by her schooling . . .

3

I Shall Keep Singing

WHEN EMILY WAS THREE, Grandfather Dickinson, badly in need of money, sold his half of the brick house and moved to Ohio. The child never saw him again, for he died five years later. Sharing a home with strangers was hard on everyone. But after seven years, Edward was able to move the family to a house of their own on what is now called North Pleasant Street.

It was a large frame house, sitting on 2 acres (less than 1 hectacre) of land. There was lots of room for a garden, an orchard, and a small grove of pine trees. Many guests would stay there, relatives, friends, and student boarders—for long or short periods. Emily and the other children sometimes shared their beds with them. In winter the bedrooms were not heated, and Emily enjoyed snuggling to keep warm. In this house Emily would live for fifteen years, finishing school and reaching into her mid-twenties.

Mr. Dickinson would never depart from the path he chose when a young man. "I do not desire a life of pleasure," he said

The frame house occupied by the Dickinsons from 1840 until 1855, when Emily was in her mid-twenties. (The porch in the photograph was added at a later date.)

then. "I anticipate pleasure from engaging with my whole soul in business." While masses of Americans were migrating west and south, he kept the family in Amherst. The editor Horace Greeley told young Americans to "go west and grow up with the country." But the Dickinsons weren't listening. They were intensely centered on home. Later, when Emily was asked if she desired anything beyond what Amherst could offer, her answer was, "I don't care for roving."

At the age of five, Emily began primary school. It was in a two-story brick building, with a woodshed and a privy outside. She learned reading and writing and some simple arithmetic. Spelling too, of course, but the standard way would never appeal to her. Her mother also spelled poorly, and was careless about punctuation. Drilling was the method teachers followed. The children learned by heart bits of information, then spouted them back to the teacher. Much later, recalling the time when a teacher put her in a closet because of some little misdeed—perhaps chattering in class—Emily wrote these verses:

> They shut me up in Prose—
> As when a little Girl
> They put me in a Closet—
> Because they like me "still"—
>
> Still! Could themself have peeped—
> And seen my Brain—go round—
> They might as wise have lodged a Bird
> For Treason—in the Pound—
>
> Himself has but to will
> And easy as a Star
> Look down upon Captivity—
> And laugh—No more have I—

Even before starting school, Emily showed her love for music. An aunt remembered her when still only two and a half, banging on the piano and talking about her "moosic." Attending church as a child, she heard and sang hymns. She studied voice at a local singing school as well. Many songbooks, both religious and secular, were found in home and in school in those days. Later, at fifteen, she took piano lessons, practicing two hours a day.

The sound of music would one day be heard in her poetry. Often she spoke of poetry as music, as song:

I shall keep singing!
Birds will pass me
On their way to Yellower Climes—
Each—with a Robin's expectation—
I—with my Redbreast—
And my Rhymes—

Late—when I take my place in summer—
But—I shall bring a fuller tune—
Vespers—are sweeter than Matins—Signor—
Morning—only the seed of Noon.

At home, or away at sessions of the Massachusetts legislature, to which he was elected in 1847, Edward kept close watch on his children's progress in school. When Emily was seven he wrote them, "Keep school, and learn, so as to tell me, when I come home, how many new things you have learned, since I came away." And again, "I want to have you do perfectly right—always be kind & pleasant, & always tell the truth, & never deceive. That is the way to become good . . . so that you can teach others to do right."

And then he let them know how lucky they were to be Dickinsons and well-off: "You have enough to eat and drink & good clothes—& go to school—while a great many poor little children have to go hungry—and have ragged clothes—& sleep cold, & have poor green wood to burn, & can't have books or go to school."

Unlike the Dickinson family, many Americans were suffering in that time from America's first economic depression. It started in 1837, with great businesses collapsing, banks and factories closing, mechanics and laborers losing their jobs. Prices of food and fuel shot up. Desperate people rioted in the streets. The effects of the depression would linger for nearly seven years.

In the first decade of Emily's life, events of explosive force occurred that barely registered in sleepy Amherst of the 1830s. The anti-slavery movement was ignited by the launching of several newspapers such as *The Liberator* and *Freedom's Advocate*. The earliest argument against racial prejudice was made powerfully by Lydia Maria Child in her *An Appeal in Favor of That Class of Americans Called Africans.* Pro-slavery mobs south and north rioted in streets and meeting halls to suppress abolitionist voices. In Virginia, Nat Turner led a slave revolt that left fifty-five whites dead and several slaves hanged.

The 1830s also saw the systematic removal of eastern Indian tribes to territory beyond the Mississippi River. In 1838, under President Andrew Jackson, 25,000 Cherokee Indians were forced out of their southeastern homes and driven on a "Trail of Tears" into exile and death.

This 1835 lithograph shows William Lloyd Garrison, a staunch abolitionist, being dragged through the streets of Boston by an angry mob.

Mr. Dickinson, however, was able to send Emily, at age nine, to an excellent private school: Amherst Academy, which her grandfather had helped to found. It took both boys and girls. For each term of eleven weeks the tuition was five dollars for the classical department, and four dollars more for the English department. Not much, considering today's great costs for private schooling. Still, it was an expense not many Amherst parents in those hard times could afford. Emily's first joy in learning came from her experience at the academy. She studied there for seven years, making several close friends among the one hundred pupils who attended.

A portrait of the three Dickinson children shows Emily at left at the age of nine. Her brother, Austin, is ten, and Lavinia is seven.

4

Opening Her Eyes

THE ACADEMY BENEFITED by its closeness to Amherst College, only three blocks away. The college provided the school with many skilled and devoted teachers. In addition, the college welcomed academy students to its lectures. The sciences were taught in both the academy and the college, and by teachers said to be the equal of any at Harvard or Yale. Courses included chemistry, botany, zoology, geography, and astronomy.

While half her studies were scientific, the other courses included ancient history, English grammar and composition, and lessons in drawing and painting. The Classical Department offered readings in the works of Caesar, Virgil, Cicero, and of course the Bible.

Emily not only learned much but often had fun doing it. At twelve, writing to a friend, she told of one young man who read a composition whose subject was "think twice before you speak." "He was describing the reasons why anyone should do so—one was—if a young gentleman—offered a young lady his arm and he

Amherst Academy, on the hill to the right, looks down over the village of Amherst. The academy provided Emily with a sound and stimulating education between 1840 and 1847. One teacher remembered her as an excellent scholar whose "compositions were strikingly original."

had a dog who had no tail and he boarded at the tavern think twice before you speak. Another is if a young gentleman knows a young lady who he thinks nature has formed to Perfection let him remember that roses conceal thorns he is the sillyest creature that ever lived I think. I told him that I thought he had better think twice before he spoke."

The academy stressed special attention "to the formation of a moral and social, as well as the intellectual character" of the pupils. They were held to high standards, but never was there any report of youngsters being abused or bullied by the teachers, in class or out.

No wonder that whenever Emily spoke of her teachers, it was always with affection, as though they were intimate friends, not remote figures whom she feared. "I am always in love with my teachers," she said.

One of them, Daniel Fiske, many years later remembered Emily "as a very bright, but rather delicate and frail-looking girl; an excellent scholar, of exemplary deportment, faithful in all school duties; but somewhat shy and nervous. Her compositions were strikingly original, and in both thought and style seemed beyond her years, and always attracted much attention in the school and, I am afraid, excited not a little envy."

It was while at the academy that Emily began to feel the close presence of death. "People are always dying here," said one neighbor. In February 1844 the mothers of two of Emily's school-mates died of tuberculosis, and soon after, a third friend lost her mother. The most terrible loss came when Emily's friend, Sophia Holland, fell sick with typhus. Emily visited her often and watched over her sickbed. As Sophia neared death, the doctor said no one but the nurse must see her. But at length he relented and let Emily take off her shoes and steal silently into the sick-room: "There she lay mild & beautiful as in health and her pale features lit up with an unearthly—smile . . . She was too lovely for earth & she was transplanted from earth to heaven," Emily wrote a friend. Such deep melancholy seized Emily that her worried parents sent her to visit her beloved Aunt Lavinia in Boston for a month.

Even worse occurred shortly after Emily's return home, when the depressed wife of a family friend killed herself.

Struggling to overcome her grief, Emily resumed her studies at the academy. One of the textbooks used in class, Parker's *Aids to English Composition*, offers some clues to Emily's way of writing.

For instance, her liberal use of the dash, in both her poems and letters. Parker wrote:

> The proper use of the dash is to express a sudden stop, or change of the subject; but, by modern writers, it is employed as a substitute for almost all the other marks; being sometimes used for a comma, semicolon, colon, or period; sometimes for a question or an exclamation and sometimes for crotchets and brackets to enclose a parenthesis.

Emily must have been encouraged by what Parker said up front in his book:

> Genius cannot be fettered, and an original and thinking mind, replete with its own exuberance, will often burst out in spontaneous gushings, and open itself to new channels, through which the treasures of thought will flow in rich and rapid currents.

She would often use the dash to gain rhythm and emphasis. She also felt free to use capital letters to gain emphasis.

Here is one example, where Emily tells us what the release from school at noon on Saturdays felt like:

> From all the Jails the Boys and Girls
> Ecstatically leap—
> Beloved only afternoon
> That Prison doesn't keep—
>
> They storm the Earth and stun the Air,
> A Mob of solid Bliss—
> Alas—that Frowns should lie in wait
> For such a Foe as this—

Emily had no trouble making friends while at school. At thirteen, she was one of a group of girls called "The Five." Friends noted later that she was quick to attach herself to others, and to hang on to them long after. Her sister Lavinia said that far from being "withdrawn or reclusive," Emily was "always looking for the rewarding person to come." Among her group she was the one who did most to keep the friendships alive, even many years after her friends had moved away from Amherst.

Emily's neighbors would come to admire her gardening, more visible evidence of her love for beauty than the poems few would see until after her death. She learned much from a textbook used in school, *Familiar Lectures in Botany*, written by Mrs. Almira Phelps. In a graceful style, Mrs. Phelps provided many hints for the dedicated gardener Emily was becoming. Like Parker's text, hers showed a fervent love for the art she helped others to create:

> The vegetable world offers a boundless field of inquiry, which may be explored with the most pure and delightful emotions. Here the Almighty seems to manifest himself to us . . . The study of botany naturally leads to greater love and reverence for the Deity . . .

What the academy did for Emily, says her biographer Richard Sewall, "was to open her eyes, give her a discipline, and set her studies in the largest possible frame of reference. Perhaps the most important thing was opening her eyes. . . ."

Emily graduated from the academy in August 1847. A month later she entered Mount Holyoke Female Seminary.

5

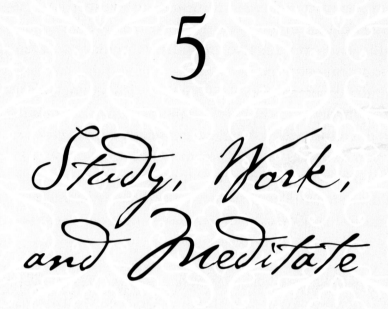

Study, Work, and Meditate

MOUNT HOLYOKE FEMALE SEMINARY had been founded only ten years before Emily entered. It was an island of female education in the New England countryside, 9 miles (14 kilometers) south of her Amherst home. Here young women could evade the tight hold of family and community. Now they were free to build new friendships.

The school aimed to fit the daughters of well-off farmers and country professionals for the work of teaching and for a life of Christian service. Many of the students would marry ministers and travel to strange continents for missionary work among the native peoples.

To enter the seminary, Emily had to take placement exams. She passed them easily. Higher education for women was only just getting under way at that time. Few teachers in such schools had advanced training, did research, or wrote texts. The door to the professions was closed to women. How could they hope to win leadership in any respected field? Remember that women could not even vote. (Not until 1920 would a constitutional amendment permit it.)

But the woman who created and headed Mount Holyoke had a vision that life could be different. Mary Lyon, a brilliant and devout educator, wanted to create the kind of school that could develop women's minds, broaden their outlook, and prepare them to be wives, teachers, and missionaries.

The courses Emily took included the sciences, geometry, chemistry, physiology, and astronomy. Every day she practiced

This lithograph of Mount Holyoke Female Seminary is based on an 1845 drawing. (It was rendered by Nathan Currier, later of Currier and Ives fame.)

The success of Mary Lyon in founding Mount Holyoke opened the doors of higher education for women. She proved that women were as intellectually capable as men, and that an institution for women offering a college curriculum could survive financially.

singing and the piano, and participated in calisthenics. And she had to write a composition every two weeks.

What her school life was like is best conveyed through an enthusiastic letter she sent her friend Abiah Root only a few weeks after classes began:

I room with my Cousin Emily, who is a Senior. She is an excellent room-mate & does all in her power to make me happy. You can imagine how pleasant a good room-mate is, for you have been away to school so much. Everything is pleasant & happy here & I think I could be no happier at any other school away from home. Things seem much more like home than I anticipated & the teachers are all very kind & affectionate to us. They call on us frequently & urge us to return their calls & when we do, we always receive a cordial welcome from them.

I will tell you my order of time for the day, as you were so kind as to give me your's. At 6. oclock, we all rise. We breakfast at 7. Our study hours begin at 8. At 9. we all meet in Seminary Hall, for devotions. At 10 3/4. I recite a review of Ancient History, in connection with which we read Goldsmith & Grimshaw. At.11. I recite a lesson in "Pope's Essay on Man" which is merely transposition. At 12. I practice Calisthenics & at 12 1/4 read until dinner, which is at 12 1/2 & after dinner, from 1 1/2 until 2 I sing in Seminary Hall. From 2 3/4 until 3 3/4. I practise upon the Piano. At 3 3/4 I go to Sections, where we give in all our accounts for the day, including, Absence—Tardiness—Communications—Breaking Silent Study hours—Receiving Company in our rooms & ten thousand other things, which I will not take time or place to mention. At 4 1/2. we go into Seminary Hall, & receive advice from Miss. Lyon in the form of a lecture. We have Supper at 6. & silent-study hours from then until the retiring bell, which rings at 8 3/4, but the tardy bell does not ring until 9 3/4, so that we dont often obey the first warning to retire.

Unless we have a good & reasonable excuse for failure upon any of the items, that I mentioned above, they are recorded & a black mark stands against our names: As you can easily imagine, we do not like very well to get "exceptions" as they are called scientifically here.

The students were required to do the domestic work, chores Emily didn't mind. She was used to it at home, and would continue doing it all her life:

> The domestic work is not difficult & consists in carrying the Knives from the 1st tier of tables at morning & noon & at night washing and wiping the same quantity of Knives. I am quite well & hope to be able to spend the year here, free from sickness. You have probably heard many reports of the food here & if so I can tell you, that I have yet seen nothing corresponding to my ideas on that point from what I have heard. Everything is wholesome & abundant & much nicer than I should imagine could be provided for almost 300 girls. We have also a great variety upon out tables & frequent changes. One thing is certain & that is, that Miss. Lyon & all the teachers, seem to consult our comfort & happiness in everything they do & you know that is pleasant. When I left home, I did not think I should find a companion or a dear friend in all the multitude. I expected to find rough & uncultivated manners, & to be sure, I have found some of that stamp, but on the whole, there is an ease & grace & desire to make one another happy, which delights & at the same time, surprises me very much. I find no Abby. or Abiah. or Mary, but I love many of the girls.
>
> Austin came to see me when I had been here about two weeks & brought Viny & Abby. I need not tell you how delighted I was to see them all, nor how happy it made me to hear them say that "they were so lonely." It is a sweet feeling to know that you are missed & that your memory is precious at home.

Study, work—and meditate. Twice each day, half-hour periods were set aside for solitary meditation and prayer. Miss Lyon believed not only in the duty and dignity of labor but in the great power of each of the girls "to become almost what we will."

Emily didn't neglect her music. A classmate, Amelia Jones (later Mrs. George L. Stearns), who, like Emily, had sung in the church choir back home, recalled how much she missed it. One day Emily came into Amelia's room, singing-book in hand, and urged her to come along. They walked outdoors for a while,

> Then, perched upon the topmost rail of a fence, we opened the book and our mouths, drew the diapason stops of our vocal organs, and sang tune after tune,—long metres, short metres, hallelujah metres, et id omne genus,—chants rounds, fugues, anthems, etc. etc., carrying two parts, and by snatches three or four, as the score demanded. We sang and sang till the valley rang "with our hymns of lofty cheer." Our only visible auditors were two or three cows that had been quietly feeding in a pasture near. They were too well-bred to obtrude with double-bass bellowing or with horn accompaniment, but they ceased their cropping and stood in silent amazement at the unusual sight and sound. We needed no plaudits, for we were a joy to ourselves. We had found a remedy for depression, repression, suppression and oppression, and no two maidens returned that day from open-air exercises more exhilarated than we. The seminary choirs were ere long arranged for regular practise, which was the tonic and safety valve we needed.

A collection of Emily's sheet music survives. It shows how familiar she was with a wide range of popular songs—waltzes, marches, quicksteps. It includes "Ethiopian Melodies" too, with lyrics from the minstrel shows that toured the country. Two of her songs came from the Hutchinson Family, a popular troupe known for their abolition music. She heard Haydn's oratorio *The Creation* at a concert, and also the international singing star Jenny Lind. Once she told a visitor that after listening to a great concert pianist, "she had become convinced that she could never master

My Own Words So Chill and Burn Me

In a letter to a friend, Emily wrote that when a little girl she thought "that words were cheap and weak. Now I don't know of anything so mighty . . . Sometimes I write and look at his outlines till he glows as no sapphire . . . My own words so chill and burn me."

Surely her love for words and their power was nourished by her wide reading from early on. A partial list of favorite authors would include Emily and Charlotte Brontë, Charles Dickens, Henry David Thoreau, Ralph Waldo Emerson, and of course William Shakespeare, her most-beloved author. Of George Eliot (the pseudonym of Mary Ann Evans) she said, "She is the lane to

Emily Dickinson's Bible, a gift from her father in 1844, bears evidence of lifelong use. The turned corners are in the Book of Revelation.

the Indies, Columbus was looking for." Eliot believed men and women had different voices, and that women should not fit themselves into the literary mold man made for them. From *Kavanaugh,* a novel by Longfellow, Emily absorbed the advice of the title character: "What is best for us lies always within reach, though often overlooked . . . We can give to others only what we have."

In 1851 a sensational novel, *Uncle Tom's Cabin,* began to appear in a newspaper, printed weekly just as each chapter came from the pen of Harriet Beecher Stowe. In book form a year later, the anti-slavery novel was a sensational best seller. But to her father, Emily said, it was a "nothing." Whether Emily ever read it, we don't know.

In her early twenties, Emily read Elizabeth Barrett Browning's essay, "A Vision of Poets." In it the British poet compared poetry to Scripture, in that poets too served humanity as saints and martyrs. Some of Emily's later poems would present the suffering poet as the central figure.

And the King James Bible—it was of the greatest influence from her earliest years. When her father was home, he began every morning by reading from it in his resonant voice, and then leading the family in prayer. Emily grew up knowing the Bible almost by heart. She would quote from it or refer to it often in both her poetry and prose. Its rhythms, its images, its stories, its characters enriched her life and her language.

Her own Bible, pocket-size and in tiny print, is in the Houghton Library at Harvard. Between pages 286 and 287 is a pressed clover from her father's grave.

Yet Emily ignored several great writers of her time—Nathaniel Hawthorne, Walt Whitman, Herman Melville. This, while enjoying many of the far less talented writers whose books and magazine pieces were so enormously popular.

the art and had forthwith abandoned it once and for all, giving herself up then wholly to literature."

Emily stayed at the seminary for only her first two terms, or about a year. No one is sure why. Perhaps because she was weakened by a cough that winter, which got so bad she had to go home for a while to recover. And maybe her parents thought it better for her health not to have her go on with her studies away from home. Plus, she was homesick off and on.

There was also her feeling about the steady religious pressure upon the students. Miss Lyon sermonized at the assembly three times every week, urging upon the girls a commitment to Christ. Her sermons and thos of visiting preachers bored Emily, thrilled her, or even scared her. Her pious cousin and roommate, Emily Norcross, told a friend that Emily "says she has no particular objection to becoming a Christian and she says she feels bad when she hears of one and another of her friends who are expressing a hope, but still she feels no more interest."

There were many other girls like her. Of the 230 students enrolled in Emily's year at the seminary, about half began as not established Christians, and thirty, including Emily, ended the year in the same state of mind.

Professor Sewall thought that Amherst Academy may have given Emily "all the formal education she needed or wanted." But her time in Amherst went beyond formal education and seems to have provided the good earth needed for genius to flower.

6

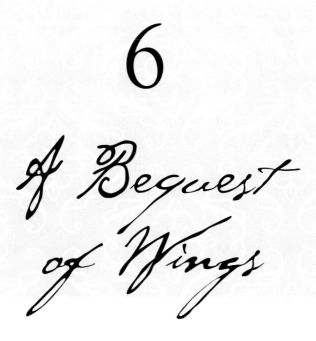

WHAT WOULD SHE DO now that she'd left the seminary? Become a teacher? A missionary? These were not for her. Nor was she drawn to social reform, even though the first stirrings of a women's movement were plainly visible. The very year after she left Mount Holyoke, the first women's rights convention was held at Seneca Falls, New York. Some two hundred people gathered to issue their own Declaration of Independence, declaring that "all men *and women* are created equal." They demanded that women be given their full political and civil rights as citizens of the United States.

Close by the Dickinsons, in Worcester, Massachusetts, the national women's rights movement was launched in 1850. These feminists (a term not yet coined) were rejecting everything their society told them about women. And that even included Mary Lyon, the founder of Mt. Holyoke. Although Miss Lyon encouraged her students to become teachers and missionaries, she also told them how valuable their domestic training was. "O how

The American feminist movement is said to have been launched with the fiery rhetoric of Elizabeth Cady Stanton and others at the 1848 Seneca Falls Convention. Such public expression would have been painful for Dickinson, yet she was quietly making her own inroads into the predominantly male world of poetry.

immensely important is this work of preparing the daughters of the land to be good mothers!" The convention called for women's social, economic, political, and moral equality with men. Why teach only daughters to cook and sew and clean? Housework wasn't destined only for females!

Many community leaders spoke loudly and repeatedly against any woman "daring to step forth and assume the duties of the man." One pastor denounced that woman whose "voice is heard from house to house . . . rising in harsh unnatural tones of denunciation against civil laws and rulers . . . expecting to reform politics and churches, and to put down every real and supposed evil in them, by the right arm of female power."

Most of these "agitators" came from the middle class, as did the Dickinsons. But they wanted to speak for their poorer sisters too. They were rejecting traditional teachings that male dominance is natural, God-given, and universal. They believed that this way of thinking had to be ended, for the benefit of men and women alike.

In Northampton, only 10 miles (16 kilometers) from Amherst, a utopian commune had sprung up. Social and racial equality were among its ideals, and people the Dickinsons knew were resident members. Yet we have no record of family interest in it. Possibly because such letters may have been lost or destroyed.

The domestic limits placed on the vast majority of women inevitably affected the kind of writing they did. In 1848–1849 two popular collections of women's poetry appeared. The verses were polite and sentimental. The poets didn't think of themselves as professional authors. For middle-class women, earning their living by the pen wasn't the right thing to do.

Their work appeared frequently in many newspapers and magazines. Their focus, wrote the scholar Paul Bennett, "was on the duties and obligations, the joys and sorrows, of domestic existence. They celebrate life's small triumphs and God's great beneficence." Only rarely did any of them challenge the injustices done the Native Americans, the slaves, or the masses of working people.

It was in late 1849 that Emily received a gift of Emerson's *Poems*, given to her by Benjamin F. Newton, who studied law with her father. Nine years older than Emily, he helped shape her growth and was the first person to encourage her as a writer. She admired him for "the strength and grace of an intellect far surpassing my own." He taught her, she said, "what to read, what authors to admire, what was most grand or beautiful in nature, and that sublimer lesson, a faith in things unseen and in a life again, nobler, and much more blessed."

What she learned from reading Emerson was to trust herself. He believed common sense isn't everything. To the creative mind nothing is closed. No institution or precedent or preachment is beyond challenge.

The effect of the right book reaching the right mind at just the right moment is voiced in one of Emily's poems:

> He ate and drank the precious Words—
> His Spirit grew robust—
> He knew no more that he was poor,
> Nor that his frame was Dust—
> He danced along the dingy Days
> And this Bequest of Wings
> Was but a Book—What Liberty
> A loosened spirit brings—

Just as influential was Charlotte Brontë's novel *Jane Eyre,* lent to Emily around this time. The heroine's character underscored the values of Emerson: "to look within one's self rather than to the world without for motives and rules of action."

Early in 1850 Emily got her first and only dog, a big animal she named Carlo. He always went along with her on walks and visits. Probably it was her father's way of protecting her when he was away from home. Carlo would be her companion for the next sixteen years, until he died.

Once, jokingly, she sent someone a prose valentine in the name of Carlo. In the midst of it Carlo declares, "The Dog is the noblest work of Art, sir. I may safely say the noblest—his mistress's rights he doth defend—although it bring him to his end—although to death it doth him send!"

Of all the family, says Sewall, her brother, Austin, "was closest to Emily in temperament, taste, sense of self and of the world." They shared a sense of humor (as well as considerable inner turmoil). Like his father and grandfather, he became a power in Amherst College and in almost every civic and business enterprise in the town. He would rove the countryside to find just the right trees and shrubs to beautify the town. He had the money to buy the paintings and rare old books he loved, and to keep fine horses.

And like Emily, he could write letters of such quality that lucky recipients prized them. He went often to the theater and to concerts during his stays in Boston.

Emily wrote him whenever he was away, saying how much she missed him and longed to hear his happy voice. "There was always such a Hurrah wherever you was," she wrote when she was just eleven.

The few letters between them that survive suggest the flights of fancy that delighted them. "What makes a few of us so different from the others?" she wrote him. "It's a question I often ask myself." Austin was her mainstay, until he married Susan Gilbert and they moved into the house next door.

When Austin graduated from Amherst College in 1850, he tried teaching in Boston for about a year, but didn't take to it. He

Emily Dickinson's brother, Austin, shown here in 1854 before his marriage to Susan, was Emily's intellectual companion and confidant.

couldn't deal with the Irish children who were flooding the schools, their families driven to emigrate by the devastating potato famine at home. Unhappy, he quit teaching and entered Harvard Law School. After graduating he became his father's law partner and stayed in Amherst the rest of his life.

His spirits seems to have slipped downward, year after year. Maybe if he went west, like so many other young hopefuls, life would be happier? But he decided not to. When his father offered to build a fine new home next door for him and Susan, he couldn't say no.

Austin's closeness to Emily may have been a factor in that decision. For he depended on his extraordinary sister, not only for intellectual companionship, but for her warm concern for his well-being. She knew how moody, how unhappy he could be at times, and was always quick to try to bolster his spirits.

Emily obviously approved of her brother's marriage to Susan Gilbert. She and Susan were close friends and, indeed, Emily wrote a poem in honor of Susan's joining their family.

The Iron Horse

Emily Dickinson was born just a few years after the first railroad began operating in America. It was 1827 when that train ran on wooden tracks from the granite quarries of Quincy, Massachusetts, to the Neponset River. A 3-mile (5-kilometer) haul! But what an uproar it caused! No one yet understood how profound a change the invention of the railroad would create in world history.

Edward Dickinson early on grasped how the railroad would improve commerce and trade and began a lobbying campaign to

This illustration of one of the earliest trains captures the ambiance created when an "iron horse" moved through the quite countryside. Emily Dickinson was able to express that feeling in words.

bring a branch line to Amherst. That first attempt failed. But he didn't give up. In 1850, when a line running north to New Canaan, Connecticut, reached nearby Palmer, he renewed the battle to finance an extension of that line to Amherst, and then on to connect with an existing line.

In 1852 enough shares had been sold to investors for construction to begin. Mr. Dickinson had accomplished two great changes in Amherst history: the development of the college and the building of the railroad. That triumph set Emily crowing about "the victory of heroic fathers."

Later, she wrote a poem in which a spectator watches an iron horse have its own way moving through the land:

I like to see it lap the Miles—
And lick the Valleys up—
And stop to feed itself at Tanks—
And then—prodigious step
Around a Pile of Mountains—
And supercilious peer
In Shanties—by the sides of Roads—
And then a Quarry pare
To fit its Ribs
And crawl between
Complaining all the while
In horrid—hooting stanza—
Then chase itself down Hill—
And neigh like Boanerges—
Then—punctual as a Star
Stop—docile and omnipotent
At its own stable door—

It was soon after Emily's return home from the seminary that Austin had begun courting Susan. The path to their marriage in 1856 was not smooth. In one of his letters to her, Austin said, "I never did, and dont now think we understand one another."

Susan had been born only a few days after Emily. She was the daughter of Harriet and Thomas Gilbert, of Deerfield, Massachusetts. Two years later her family moved to Amherst, where Susan's father took over the Mansion House, an inn and stagecoach stop. Orphaned early, Susan moved in and out of town, to stay with relatives or attend school. The two girls don't seem to have become friends until their late teens. When Austin began courting Susan in 1850, she and Emily started a lifelong intimate correspondence. There are far more letters of Emily's to Susan than to any other person.

Susan, pretty, outspoken, independent, ambitious, had become a star of the younger Amherst crowd. She and Austin had been dating since Austin's senior year at college, with Austin more passionate in his attachment than she seemed to be. Judging by Susan's letters to her brothers during the courtship, she viewed marriage to Austin as a practical matter. Every girl expected to marry. Here she was, born into a tavern keeper's family, orphaned early on, and in comes this man from the town's elite, offering her a fine new home of her own.

So they married, and Susan made their home, called the Evergreens, the center of social life. When distinguished visitors, like Emerson, came to lecture, Austin and Sue entertained them. Emily often went next door to enjoy "my crowd" as she put it. But for Austin, Sue's expensive teas, dinners, and dancing parties became a burden. More and more often he found excuses to be absent on such occasions.

Perhaps even more important in Emily's life than Austin was her sister, Vinnie. She was the Dickinson who could be depended upon by the whole family for everyday needs and in major crises.

Emily's sister, Lavinia, "Vinnie," was of a much sprightlier nature than Emily. Despite Vinnie's more active social life, they both remained unmarried and lived together at the family homestead.

It was Vinnie's lifelong devotion to her sister that rescued for the world the poems that would otherwise have been lost.

The sisters played together as children—they were only two years apart—and as they grew older, Emily came to depend upon Vinnie for help in practical matters. When in their teens, it was Vinnie who led the more active social life. She fell in love more than once, and marriage to one or two of her beaus seemed in the offing. But for whatever reason, it never came about. And Vinnie, like Emily, remained a spinster.

As she grew into maturity, Vinnie developed into the staunchest protector of the Dickinsons. She would hear no criticism of any of them. You were either a Friend of the family, or a Foe. For Emily she proved to be a stabilizing influence, a sister who would look after the details in matters great or small. Once, when Vinnie was ill for a time with headaches, Emily wrote friends that "Vinnie is sick tonight, which gives the world a russet tinge, usually so red. It is only a headache, but when the head aches next to you, it becomes important. When she is well, time leaps. When she is ill, he lags, or stops entirely."

7

Valentine's Day

IT IS FROM HER LATE TEENS that we have the first evidence of Emily's writing poems. You could see her intense concern for words and how best to use them in letters written much earlier. Teachers praised her schoolgirl compositions, but we have none of them. Her letters gradually shed stock phrases and clichés and become tighter and even satiric. Writing to Austin in 1847, when the Mexican War was nearing its end, she asked, "Has the Mexican War terminated yet & how? Are we beat? Do you know of any nation about to besiege South Hadley?" It hints that she knew of the burning opposition by many to what they considered a predatory war against Mexico, whose real goal was to grab more territory for American slaveholders.

Valentines sent in verse were common then. Schoolgirls loved to turn them out. At Mount Holyoke, Miss Lyon issued an edict against them, which Emily ignored.

To Leonard Humphrey, the principal of Amherst Academy, a bachelor ten years her senior, Emily in 1850 sent a verse valentine. It was submitted to the Amherst College paper and was the first of her poems to be published. Mating, it says, is the law of life. One stanza offers a list of eligible maidens:

> There's Sarah, and Eliza, and Emeline so fair,
> And Harriet, and Susan, and she with curling hair!
> Thine eyes are sadly blinded, but yet thou mayest see
> Six true, and comely maidens sitting upon the tree . . .

The valentine closes by urging the choice of one:

> Then bear her to the greenwood, and build for her a bower
> And give her what she asketh, jewel, or bird, or flower.
> And bring the fife, and trumpet, and beat upon the drum—
> And bid the world Goodmorrow, and go to glory home!

One of her valentines, very long, was her first verse to be published in the *Springfield Republican*. No one knows who sent it in, but it appeared in the newspaper's February 20, 1852, issue. Here are the last three quatrains:

> Good bye, sir, I am going;
> My country calleth me;
> Allow me Sir, at parting,
> To wipe my weeping e'e.

> In token of our friendship
> Accept this "Bonnie Doon,"
> And when the hand that plucked it
> Hath passed beyond the moon,

> The memory of my ashes
> Will consolation be;
> Then farewell, Tuscarora,
> And farewell, Sir, to thee!

In a letter to Austin in 1853, she speaks of being "in the habit myself of writing some few things." In another letter she confides to her friend Jane Humphrey, "I have dared to do strange things—bold things, and have asked no advice from any . . . and life has had an aim, and the world has been too precious."

Those words could have referred to a love affair, but Sewall believes they speak of "her joy in the prospect of a poetic vision— a vision of a world that she as a poet could create—that has made all things new for her."

About ten years later, she wrote a poem that tells us what comes first in a poet's world:

I reckon—when I count at all—
First—Poets—Then the Sun—
Then Summer—Then the Heaven of God—
And then—the List is done—

But, looking back—the First so seems
To Comprehend the Whole—
The Others look a needless Show—
So I write—Poets—All

Their Summer—lasts a Solid Year—
They can afford a Sun
The East—would deem extravagant—
And if the Further Heaven—

Be Beautiful as they prepare
For those who worship Them—
It is too difficult a Grace—
To justify the Dream—

Were there young men in Emily's life? Any love affairs? We can't be sure, the evidence is so scanty. Only a small fraction of the letters Emily wrote have come down to us, and a much smaller number of those written to her. There's no doubt that young men at Amherst College dropped in often on the Dickinsons. They took the sisters on sleigh rides, to lectures and concerts. Yet only scraps of information exist to tell us how the young people felt about one another, how casually or deeply.

Mr. Dickinson's law students were naturally welcomed in the family. We've met Ben Newton, whom Emily herself described as so important to her development. But he was more an older brother than a suitor. Close by at the college were two other young men whose friendship she cherished. One was John Graves, a distant cousin who would graduate with high honors. He came often to call. And she would entertain him by playing the piano. Sometimes she improved "weird and beautiful melodies," a talent she exercised especially at night, and the later the better.

Emily wrote in 1852 of finding "a beautiful new friend" in Henry Vaughan Emmons, a college friend of Graves's. She went out riding with him, he called on her many evenings, and they exchanged books and flowers. Although he had run away from home in Maine when a youngster, now he had become an honored scholar at the college. She seems to have favored him with a few of her early poems in manuscript. But there is no hint that their friendship ever deepened into love. He married many years later.

Many others came to visit Emily or Vinnie. If Emily felt romantic about any of them, we don't know. At any rate, it was not her nature to be gushy. Some who came to call she dismissed as boring, dull, or egotistic. Scholars have held that Emily's father scared off potential suitors. But he seems not to have been intimidating, only protective. After Emily was gone, Vinnie told a friend, "Emily never had any love disaster."

John Graves (left) was Dickinson's cousin through the Gunn side of the family. Henry Vaughan Emmons had a strong interest in literature and religion. They were two of the many young Amherst students who called at the Dickinson household to enjoy the company of the scholarly Emily and the vivacious Vinnie.

An old physical complaint threatened both Emily and Vinnie in 1851. Each was coughing a lot, and complaining of feeling sick. It was scary, for so many among family, friends and neighbors sickened and died of tuberculosis. They were examined first by one local doctor, then another, with no firm diagnosis. (In the mid-1800s, medicine was in almost a primitive stage compared with today's science.)

The sisters were taken to Boston to seek medical advice. A Harvard professor of medicine, an expert in lung disease, gave them his basic advice: to eat well and to exercise outdoors. Today, medical authorities believe Emily must have had tuberculosis of the lungs. It is an illness that can have different outcomes—it can be transitory or persist for years or kill quickly.

8

A Trip "Abroad"

EMILY SO RARELY LEFT the narrow bounds of
Amherst, that when she did, it needs special attention. It happened
when her father was elected to Congress in 1852.

Edward Dickinson's political career rose out of his role as
treasurer of Amherst College. When a great depression began, it
reduced the college's financial support. It was hoped the state
government would come to the rescue. So in 1838, Mr. Dickinson
agreed, reluctantly, to run for a seat in the Massachusetts legislature, where he would lobby for an appropriation. He served two
terms in the lower house, and was twice elected to the State
Senate. Getting deeper and deeper into politics, he was then
elected to the governor's executive council.

He gave his political energy to the Whig party. It was organ-
ized in the 1830s to oppose Jacksonian Democrats. It was a
mixed bag of many diverse points of view on what America
needed. But generally, while its voters supported the business
interests, it also was for prison reform, educational reform,

abolition of capital punishment, and temperance. You couldn't say the Whig party was anti-slavery, but free blacks and abolitionists preferred it to the fiercely pro-slavery Jacksonian Democrats. Although Jacksonians called it the party of the rich, the Whigs drew support from people of all classes.

As for Mr. Dickinson, in his college years he had spoken against slavery, and later as a lawyer, had defended three young Amherst blacks who had abducted a black orphan girl to save her from being sold into slavery.

Yet as a supporter of states' rights, he believed a federal law abolishing slavery would be unconstitutional. He knew, of course, that the U.S. Constitution recognized slavery, but he, like so many others, couldn't see that as a fatal flaw in the founding document.

That decade of the 1850s was a time when politicians both North and South were trying to stave off a direct confrontation between the slave labor and the free labor systems. The political pot had come to a boil, with both Democrats and Whigs divided into warring factions over slavery. The Compromise of 1850 had satisfied neither side, producing only an uneasy truce.

A coalition of Northerners and Easterners bolted from the old parties to form the new Republican party. The Illinois lawyer Abraham Lincoln, who like Mr. Dickinson was elected to Congress that year, and who would serve only one term, wrote:

> I think there is no peaceful extinction of slavery in prospect for us . . . Our political problem now is "Can we, as a nation, continue together permanently—forever—half slave and half free?"

Edward Dickinson too had his strong doubts. In May 1854 a meeting of all those in Congress opposed to pro-slavery legislation and interested in the formation of a new party—the Republicans—met in Dickinson's rooms in Washington.

While Father was serving in Congress, Emily and Vinnie went down to Washington to visit him. It was early in February 1855. Father was busy with legislative matters—"All is jostle here—scramble and confusion"—and there is no evidence of what he may have done with his daughters. However, from letters the sisters wrote, we know of some happenings.

They took a trip by boat to nearby Mount Vernon, the home of George Washington. Emily wrote her friend, Mrs. Holland, about how much it meant to her:

> I will not tell you what I saw—the elegance, the grandeur; you will not care to know the value of the diamonds my Lord and Lady wore, but if you haven't been to the sweet Mount Vernon, then I will tell you how on one soft spring day we glided down the Potomac in a painted boat, and jumped upon the shore— how hand in hand we stole along up a tangled pathway till we reached the tomb of General George Washington, how we paused beside it, and no one spoke a word, then hand in hand walked on again, not less wise or sad for that marble story; how we went within the door—raised the latch he lifted when he last went home—thank the Ones in Light that he's since passed in through a brighter wicket! Oh, I could spend a long day, if it did not weary you, telling of Mount Vernon—and I will sometime if we live and meet again, and God grant we shall!

Except for this excursion, there is little documentation of how they spent those three weeks in Washington. One woman who met them where they were staying at the Willard Hotel remarked that "Emily impressed me as a girl with large, warm heart, earnest nature and delicate tastes, & we soon became friends."

One of the few other things we know is that, sitting next to a judge at dinner, when the flaming plum pudding was served, she said, "Oh Sir, may one eat of hell fire with impunity here?"

But nothing she saw or did in the capital made her wish to leave Amherst more often. "For one look at you, for your gentle voices, I'd exchange it all," she wrote home. "The pomp—the court—the etiquette—they are of the earth—will not enter Heaven."

From Washington the sisters traveled homeward, stopping in Philadelphia to visit two weeks with their friend, and second cousin, Eliza Coleman. Only one letter survives from that visit, and it tells us little. There is much speculation about whether this was the time when Emily met Charles Wadsworth, minister of the Colemans' church, the Arch Street Presbyterian Church. It's likely that the sisters were taken to hear the city's most famous minister. He was forty-one then, and married. A powerful preacher, he was considered one of the best in the nation. A newspaper article

It is likely that Dickinson first encountered Reverend Charles Wadsworth at a church service in Philadelphia. She said of him, "The very appearance of the man in the pulpit shows his abhorrence of claptrap."

described him as slender; with dark eyes, hair, and complexion; with a sweet, touching voice, warmth of manner, and lively imagination. Interestingly, when young, he had been spoken of as a poetic prodigy. He could be funny too. Mark Twain, who heard him preach, reported that he would speak of those grave Sunday school books and of "the good little boys in them who always went to Heaven, and the bad little boys who infallibly got drowned on Sundays."

Wadsworth's magnetic presence, whenever they may have met, so impressed Emily that in letters later on she spoke of him as "the beloved clergyman . . . so noble . . . so gentle . . . my dearest earthly friend." Emily had two volumes of his sermons, which were rich in imagery and evidence of how widely he read. In one sermon he assailed the junk so frequently published: "Three quarters of our magazines are a poor conglomerate of pretentious platitude, pointless tales, fulsome reviews, and bedizened rhyme, made to do service as poetry."

He would visit her twice, in 1860 and again in 1880. Two years later he died. The connection between the two remains a mystery. Austin said of his sister that she "reached out eagerly, fervently even, toward anybody who kindled the spark."

In 1855, soon after returning from his only term in Congress (he lost his campaign for re-election), Mr. Dickinson bought back the Homestead. Along with it he acquired an 11-acre (5-hectare) meadow across the road. He had costly remodeling work done to ensure that his house would remain one of Amherst's finest.

Emily was given the circular bedroom on the second floor. There she wrote her poems and letters at her small desk. Atop the house was a cupola to which she climbed by a trapdoor ladder.

It was now that Mr. Dickinson induced Austin to give up any thought of leaving the town by making him his full law partner and paying to build a new home next door for him and his bride, Sue. They called it The Evergreens.

Dickinson's bedroom as it looks today. The house is owned by Amherst College and is open to the public by appointment.

The move back to the old home somehow unsettled Emily's mother. She felt dizzy, disoriented, unable to carry the household responsibility. She would lie about on the sofa or cling to her easy chair, near collapse. It was so frightening that Emily felt her own "machinery" might go out of gear.

There was just a short pathway between Susan and Austin's bustling home, the Evergreens, and the Dickinson Homestead, where Emily lived a much quieter life.

Mrs. Dickinson's breakdown lasted for years. "I know not what to hope for her," Emily said. The illness led to Emily's clinging even more closely to home. She and Vinnie took over the running of the house.

The next four years of her life would be a time of strain, both within the home and within herself.

9

Independent as the Sun

NOW IN HER MIDTWENTIES, Emily began to withdraw from friends and community. Perhaps she was digging more deeply into her self, searching for the treasures demanding expression.

Into her secluded life came Samuel Bowles, bringing with him the great world outside. He was the editor of the *Springfield Republican,* one of the best newspapers in America. His leadership in journalism brought him into close connection with momentous events and the men and women who figured in them.

It was Austin's friendship with Bowles that brought the editor into the family circle. A few years older than Austin, at seventeen he had begun working for his father, the owner of the *Republican.* Only a year later, the brash young man took over from his father the chief responsibility for the paper. He would give his life to it, moving deeply into local, state, and national politics, traveling

Samuel Bowles's vibrant personality and his "knack of drawing out plain and unattractive people" sparked a strong response in Emily Dickinson.

the country and Europe too in his successful effort to make his newspaper a progressive power in the young democracy.

Around 1856, Bowles, sometimes with his wife, Mary, began frequent visits to the home of the newlyweds, Austin and Sue. He knew Amherst well, for his paper reported on local events and personalities. And he had met Sue earlier, in her girlhood. His visits to Amherst were meant to ease the tension of his unending labors. A handsome man, whose "beautiful eyes" Emily never forgot, he was the center at social gatherings, quick at games, playful, gracious to all, with a gift for drawing people out.

As a close friend of Austin and Sue, he stayed in their home when he visited Amherst. And there he got to know Emily. While Emily began writing to his wife Mary, sending her poems and flowers, it was clear she had a special feeling for Samuel. Some think it more than that, and have called it love.

Bowles was a liberal thinker on women's rights, and published several women writers in his paper. He shared with Emily her admiration of the Brontë sisters and Elizabeth Barrett Browning.

Browning's achievement was an example to Emily of a woman making herself a great force in the world of thought and art. That a woman could be great was not what a Dickinson was raised to believe. Now Emily was coming to believe it, and in a letter to her young first cousin, Louise Norcross, she reminded her of the time when

> you and I in the dining room decided to be distinguished. It's a great thing to be "great" Loo, and you and I might tug for a life, and never accomplish it, but no one can stop our looking on, and you know some cannot sing, but the orchard is full of birds and we can all listen. What if we learn ourselves some day!

The example too of Fanny Kemble helped Emily to envision herself as some day achieving greatness. Kemble was the British actress who had won great praise for her performances in Shakespeare's plays. She had then married an American planter, owner of seven hundred slaves, and had gone to live on his Georgia plantation. Her acute observation of what daily life meant for slave families she recorded in her *Journal of a Residence on a Georgian Plantation*. It is one of the most penetrating accounts of

Dickinson admired Fanny Kemble's strong stance against slavery and her ability to speak out in public.

American slavery ever written. When conflict with her husband over her commitment to human equality between the races and between men and women ended her marriage, she began touring America, doing readings of Shakespeare's women characters. She took the critics and the public by storm.

Mr. Dickinson disdained Kemble's public career, calling her an "animal." But Emily was stirred by such examples as Browning and Kemble to think that someday, she too might stand before the world as an artist.

But how? Couldn't she get her poems into print through Bowles's newspaper? After all, he was her friend and he welcomed women writers. In fact, only a month after his first visit to Amherst, a poem of hers did appear in the *Republican*, unsigned. But someone else had sent it in, not Emily.

Why hadn't Emily? It seems she was bound by what many people of polite society in her time believed about women: that your writing is best read in private. You don't seek public exposure of your work. You write in private and you ask only your intimates—family and friends—to enjoy what you create.

Recall that authorship by 1850 was no longer a leisured pastime. It had become a profession competing for a place in the market. Emily could never get herself to accept that. For her, writing was a spiritual calling. What her imagination produced was to be shared with friends, not sold. She owned herself and could not temper her work to meet the demands of the commercial world.

Even when, many years later, another editor asked her to submit poems to his publication, she refused. And enclosed this poem:

How happy is the little Stone
That rambles in the Road alone,
And doesn't care about Careers
And Exigencies never fears—

Whose Coat of elemental Brown
A passing Universe put on,
And independent as the Sun
Associates or glows alone,
Fulfilling absolute Decree
In casual simplicity—

So though ambition was certainly there, it was beyond her to take the stage in public print.

What did Emily look like at this time? She spoke of herself as "minute. . . . I have a little shape." My size, she said, "felt small to me." A white dress of hers shows she had a petite, slim figure. One friend said Emily was like "a white moth."

10

A Choice Spirit

CLOSE STUDY OF EMILY'S LETTERS and poems leads scholars to believe she began to write regularly in the mid-1850s. She worked in her room, where her writing desk faced Main Street. Through the window looking westward she could see wayfarers on the street or people coming in and out of the frequent parties in the Evergreens. That she was no casual correspondent is clear from the early drafts of letters. She often kept these preliminary attempts to refer to in improving the style of later letters.

Unlike most of us, who live in an age when cell phones and e-mail make communication so easy and casual, she used letter writing as a workshop in the artful use of language.

If you read a collection of Emily's letters, you find that sometimes a stream of them to a friend drops off and disappears. That friend has married, moved away, been too busy raising a family to write, or perhaps died. Or Emily herself has come to feel her correspondent doesn't really understand her unique way of writing.

But the stream of her letters to Sue, her sister-in-law living next door, never lets up for long. Far more of these have survived than letters to any other correspondent. She and Sue delivered letters face-to-face, or the children or household servants carried letters and notes between the Homestead and the Evergreens. They exchanged favorite books with their letters, and Emily often sent along gifts of bread, cake, fruit, or preserves. Some of her letters to Sue are really prose poems, or drafts she hoped Sue would comment upon.

Writing could often be interrupted by household demands. Emily and Vinnie spent what felt like endless hours keeping house. Chores included cooking, cleaning, laundry, ironing, knitting, sewing. From early childhood, girls sewed. After they mastered the small stitch and the straight seam, "good girls" plied a needle day in, day out. Usually with mother and daughters in one another's company. Some women did work in stores, workshops, and fields, but far more with the needle. Often they got together in benevolent societies, plying their needles for God and the poor or, in wartime, for the soldiers. And often they gave small gifts of their needlework to one another.

Women like Emily, who had other needs to fulfill, might have resented the demands placed upon their time, but they accepted the family's authority to make those demands.

In a large household like the Homestead, housework was exhausting. A woman could work herself sick, with the family chores more than she could bear. That may have been one reason for Mrs. Dickinson's swift decline soon after the return to the Homestead.

There were Irish servants to help—women indoors, and men for work in the barn and in the fields. Among them were two women Emily was especially fond of. Margaret O'Brien would be with them for ten years, leaving to be married. And Maggie Maher

Safe in their Alabaster Chambers,
Untouched by morning -
And untouched by noon -
Lie the meek members of
the Resurrection -
Rafter of Satin - and Roof of
Stone -

Grand go the Years - in the
Crescent - above them -
Worlds scoop their Arcs -
And Firmaments - row -
Diadems - drop - and Doges -
Surrender -
Soundless as Dots - on a
Disc of Snow -

Perhaps this verse would
please you better - Sue -

Emily !

A facsimile of one of the many letters to sister-in-law Sue, this is an early draft of Dickinson's poem "Safe in Alabaster Chambers."

Have a Piece of Cake?

If Mrs. Dickinson merited high praise for at least one thing, it was her cooking. She was "a rare and delicate cook in such matters as crullers and custards," a friend recalled, and she taught her daughters everything she knew. Emily won second prize for her bread at the Agricultural Fair. Here is one example of a much-admired family recipe, for Black Cake, adapted for present-day use:

2 cups sugar
$\frac{1}{2}$ pound butter
5 eggs
$\frac{1}{4}$ cup molasses
2 cups sifted flour
$\frac{1}{2}$ tsp baking soda
1 tsp cloves

1 tsp mace
1 tsp cinnamon
$\frac{1}{2}$ tsp ground nutmeg
$\frac{1}{4}$ to $\frac{1}{2}$ cup brandy
1 pound raisins
$\frac{2}{3}$ pound currants
$\frac{2}{3}$ pound citron

Place a shallow pan of water on the bottom of the oven and preheat oven to 225°F. (Make sure that the pan contains at least an inch of water during the first 2$\frac{1}{2}$ hours of baking time.

Gradually add sugar to butter, beating until light and creamy. Add unbeaten eggs and molasses. Beat well. Resift the flour with baking soda and spices.

Beat sifted ingredients into mixture, alternately adding brandy. Stir in raisins, currents, and citron.
Divide the batter between two loaf pans lined with waxed paper or parchment.

Bake at 225°F for 3 hours. Remove pan of water for last $\frac{1}{2}$ hour.

Let loaves cool before removing from pans.

Remove waxed paper and rewrap in fresh paper.

According to the adaptor of this recipe (to be found at http://www.geocities.com/edicksinson2002/blackcake.html), the longer the cake sits in a cool, dark spot, the better it will taste. Apparently Emily Dickinson used to put hers in the cellar for a month, but modern cooks may be a bit squeamish about that.

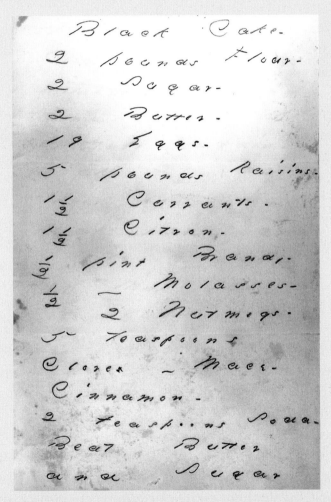

The original black cake recipe, written in Dickinson's own hand, made for quite a hearty cake, featuring two pounds each of flour, sugar, and butter, and five pounds of raisins!

stayed even longer, from 1869 till Vinnie's death in 1899. Emily spoke of Maggie as "warm and wild and mighty."

During the long New England winters, folks turned to dancing and singing schools for social life. It helped make hymns in church less noisy and more pleasing to God and the congregation. There's evidence that Emily danced too, at the Evergreens when Sue's parties provided the fun.

Emily would chat with the guests, read poetry aloud, or play on the piano a song she had composed, called "The Devil." During one boisterous evening her father, overhearing the revelry, became so upset he walked over to bring Emily home.

When a student at the academy, Emily had been in a Shakespeare club. Later she would meet with others to discuss the plays and to read aloud from them. In her letters she kept referring to the dramatist and quoting him more and more often. Shakespeare took second place in her mind only to the Bible.

Brother Austin helped enrich the town's cultural life when in 1857, with a group of young men, he formed a club to bring lecturers to Amherst, charging a very small admission so anybody could come. Among the speakers were Wendell Phillips, the noted abolitionist, and Ralph Waldo Emerson, the Concord sage and poet. Lecturers might stay overnight at Austin and Sue's, and Emily surely met them. The impression Emerson made on her led her to say it was "as if he had come from where dreams are born." Like Emerson, she would think her own thoughts and let nobody hinder them.

Of course Sam Bowles was often to be seen at the Evergreens as well. And it was good for both him and the Dickinsons. He was much closer to the ferment and tumult of those pre–Civil War years, and though the Dickinsons kept up with the news through Sam's paper, it was different to talk of it with the man from the center. Bowles in turn found rest and peace and comfort in the company of these warm friends.

Kate Turner, a young widow Sue had known at school, came several times for long visits at the Evergreens. Later she recalled what those social evenings were like:

> The blazing wood fire—Emily—Austin—the music—rampant fun—the inextinguishable laughter, the uproarious spirits of our chosen—our most congenial circle . . . Emily at the piano playing weird and beautiful melodies, all from her own inspiration. Oh! She was a choice spirit.

Emily grew very fond of Kate and wrote her fervent and funny letters. In one mailing, she sent a pair of garters she'd knit for her friend, and with it these lines:

> When Katie walks, this Simple pair accompany her side,
> When Katie runs unwearied they follow on the road,
> When Katie kneels, their loving hands will clasp her pious knee—
> Ah! Katie! Smile at Fortune, with two so knit to thee!

It was in 1858 that Emily decided to put her poems in order. These verses were often written on the backs of envelopes or brown paper bags or scraps of newspapers or discarded bills. Taking good-quality paper, she began to make clean copies of her poems. She placed several poems on each sheet, and when she'd filled four sheets, she bound them into a small booklet with needle and thread. She was using the same method as her father long before, when he preserved the pieces he'd written at college.

Such manuscript books were called fascicles, and they were not uncommon in the nineteenth century. People created their own private collections of writing they admired—stories, poems, essays, letters, often by well-known writers such as Edgar Allan

Poe. What's different about Emily's fascicles is that they were made up entirely of her own work.

Between 1858 and the end of 1865, she assembled forty of these small bundles, plus ten unthreaded others. Those she had written while a girl, she had shown or sent to other people. But most of the poems created as an adult she kept strictly to herself. Not until after her death would the family and the world learn how carefully she had preserved her work and that there were hundreds and hundreds of poems.

As people like the Dickinsons worked and played and wrote poems or made speeches, the country was coming to a boil. The Compromise of 1850 showed no sign of preventing a bloody clash between North and South over the issue of slavery. In 1857 the Supreme Court handed down the Dred Scott decision, holding that blacks "were so far inferior that they had no rights, which the white man was bound to respect."

In 1859, John Brown, with a band of twenty-one men, attacked the federal arsenal at Harpers Ferry in Virginia. He planned to seize the weapons, distribute them to the slaves, and spread a slave revolt from there across the South. The plan failed, and Brown and his men were captured. But to the enemies of slavery, the news was "high noon." Emerson said that Brown was "a new saint, who will make the gallows glorious like the cross."

Brown was tried for treason and sentenced to be hanged. In his last speech to the Virginia court, he said, "Now, if it be deemed necessary that I should forfeit my life for the furtherance of the ends of justice, and mingle my blood further with the blood of my children and with the blood of millions in this slave country whose rights are disregarded by wicked, cruel, and unjust enactments—I submit; so let it be done!"

As Brown went to his grave, the campaign for the 1860 presidential election began. The Republicans nominated Abraham

Lincoln on a platform that, though it did not call for the end of slavery, stood firmly against any further extension of the slave system.

Lincoln won (overwhelmingly in Amherst) in November, and six weeks later the South began to secede from the Union. Only five weeks after he took office, Confederate forces fired on Fort Sumter. The Civil War had begun.

What would Emily Dickinson have to say about it?

11

My Business Is to Love

THE DICKINSONS WERE NEVER set on fire by the abolitionist cause. In 1861, with the war under way, the Massachusetts Republicans wanted to put Emily's father on the ballot for lieutenant governor. He refused to run, saying publicly that he was not for "the immediate and universal emancipation of slaves." Why? Because it would violate states' rights.

A columnist on Bowles's newspaper was furious, denouncing Mr. Dickinson in print. Was he a patriot or a partisan? A liberal or a bigot? A man or a mouse? Yet Mr. Dickinson did back the North. He supported paying bounties to men who volunteered for the Union army. When Austin was drafted he paid $500 for a substitute to serve in his place.

Although many women helped the Union cause by making bandages for the wounded soldiers, Emily did not volunteer. With no one in her immediate family under fire, it would seem she felt remote from the trials and terror of men in combat. Yet at least five of her poems do touch on the war. They do not attack the South. They lament the deaths of soldiers. Her attitude to the tragedy of war is resignation.

In March 1862, Frazar Stearns, the son of the Amherst College president and a friend of Austin's, was killed in action. As he was going into the army, Emily had hoped "that ruddy face won't be brought home frozen." Frazar's death was shattering for Austin, perhaps because he felt guilty. While his friend had joined in the struggle, he had paid for a substitute. And then two more Amherst soldiers died, both of them the sons of Mrs. Adams, a professor's widow. Emily felt deeply each mother's grief, imagining a soldier's ghost "riding tonight in the mad wind—back to the village burying ground where he never dreamed of sleeping: Ah! The dreamless sleep!"

During the war, Emily spun verses that confess, privately, she wants to be famous. But not for the approval of others, only for her own:

Fame of Myself, to justify,
All other Plaudit be
Superfluous—An Incense
Beyond Necessity—

Fame of Myself to Lack—Although
My Name be else Supreme—
This were an Honor honorless—
A futile Diadem—

Two events occurred in June 1861 that gave Emily cause for joy—and for sorrow. Austin and Sue's first child was born, named Edward for his grandfather, but called Ned by everyone. Ten days later Elizabeth Barrett Browning died. Emily had loved her writing from the beginning. Her "witchcraft" had "enchanted" the young Emily, encouraging her to write. In her bedroom hung a framed portrait of the British poet.

To Sam Bowles, then touring Europe, Emily wrote, "If you touch her Grave, put one hand on the Head, for me—her unmentioned Mourner . . ."

One day in April 1862, Emily encountered a man who would mean so much to her. (Not in person, but through print.) She was reading that month's issue of the *Atlantic Monthly*. The lead essay was called "Letter to a Young Contributor." It offered practical advice to beginning writers, encouraging women and immigrants to try their hand at the basic "mystery of words." The author, Thomas Wentworth Higginson, would be an influence until long after Emily's death.

Born in Cambridge of an old Puritan family, Higginson came to Worcester, a Massachusetts town, when he was almost thirty, to be the pastor of the new Free Church. The town was an abolitionist stronghold, a key station on the Underground Railroad. (Recall it was the same town where the first national women's rights convention was held in 1850.)

Together with other local reformers who valued freedom more than law and order, Higginson was caught up in the mounting resistance to the Fugitive Slave Law of 1850. In 1854, when the runaway slave Anthony Burns was arrested in Boston and held for his Virginia master to reclaim him, it was Higginson who led a group of abolitionists in battering down the door of the courthouse to rescue Burns. But within, the constables and deputies were ready with pistols and clubs, and in the scuffle Higginson was wounded, and a deputy killed. The Massachusetts court ruled that Burns had to return to slavery.

It took a huge military force to escort Burns to the ship waiting to carry him back into bondage. As they marched Burns

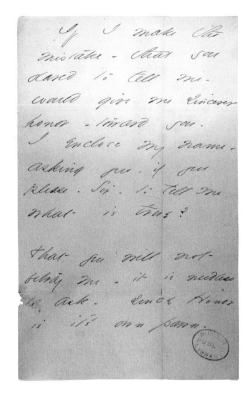

Dickinson's April 1862 letter to Reverend Thomas Wentworth Higginson began their lifelong correspondence. Instead of a signature, the poet enclosed her handwritten calling card with four poems.

through Boston to the dock, 50,000 people lined the streets, hissing and crying "Shame!"

After reading Higginson's essay on writing, Emily, now thirty-one, sent him a letter, enclosing four poems. She wanted to know what a professional literary man thought of her work, and asked him to tell her if my "verse is alive." The poems voiced her feelings about love, death, art, nature . . . subjects she often chose. "Excuse me," she wrote, "if they are untrue."

Remember that she had once said, "Truth is so rare a thing, it is delightful to tell it." The poet and critic Richard Wilbur has said

A Poem a Day

Editors have worked hard to locate the year in which each of Dickinson's poems was written, for Emily herself did not date them. It has proved so difficult a task that disagreement frequently occurs. One tally, by R. W. Franklin, holds that she composed 88 poems in 1861, 277 in 1862, 295 in 1863, and 98 in 1864. That's more than 700 poems in four years. Again, note that these are only estimates, not certainties. With so high a rate of production, it is likely that at times she wrote more than one poem a day.

In 1862 she jokingly bragged about how prolific she was:

I send Two Sunsets—
Day and I—in competition ran—
I finished Two—and several Stars—
While He—was making One—
His own was ampler—but as I
Was saying to a friend—
Mine—is the more convenient
To Carry in the Hand—

that Emily's regard for objective fact cannot be questioned. Take, for instance, her poems on the snake and the hummingbird; they are "small masterpieces of exact description." "But her chief truthfulness," he continued, "lay in her insistence on discovering the facts of her inner experience . . . describing and distinguishing the states and motions of her soul."

When Higginson took her letter from his postal box, he answered it at once. Unfortunately his letters to Emily were destroyed. We can only infer what he wrote from her replies. Although he was a reputable critic and a sound scholar, he did not then, or ever, really understand her departure from the conventional prose and verse of that time. He replied he could not recommend she publish before she had corrected her "spasmodic gait." He would ask her to use exact rhyme and grammar and punctuation the way all good writers did. And why no titles on her poems? Yet he was fascinated by the personality revealed, and would not break off the connection.

Some of Dickinson's most vital correspondences were with people she saw little of. By the mid-1870s, she had sent Higginson (shown here with daughter circa 1884) more than fifty poems, some of which he read to the New England Women's Club of Boston. He reported that "their weird and strange power excited much interest…"

Emily replied to his letter (enclosing three poems): "Thank you for the surgery—it was not so painful as I supposed. I bring you others—as you ask—though they might not differ."

In answering some questions he asked, she said, among other things:

> I have a Brother and Sister—My Mother does not care for thought—and Father, too busy with his Briefs—to notice what we do—He buys me many books but begs me not to read them—because he fears they joggle the Mind. They are religious, except me—and address an Eclipse, every morning— whom they call their "Father." But I fear my story fatigues you— I would like to learn—Could you tell me how to grow—or is it unconveyed—like Melody—or Witchcraft?

Was this thumbnail sketch of her family accurate? Not literally, but it suggests how she saw them at times.

She knew that Higginson did not think her poems were ready for publication. But she continued to write him, for plainly he cared about her ideas and her work. Now she sent him not her earlier work, but more recently composed poems. "Are these more orderly?" His reassurance meant so much that several years later she told him, "You were not aware that you saved my Life."

Wanting to know what this strange lady looked like, Higginson asked her to send him a photograph. She replied, "I had no portrait, now, but am small, like the Wren, and my Hair is bold, like the Chestnut Bur—and my eyes, like the Sherry in the Glass, that the Guest leaves—Would this do just as well?"

Then, in a word of caution, lest he misinterpret her poems, she added: "When I state myself, as the Representative of the Verse—it does not mean—me—but a supposed person."

About the same time, writing to her friends, the Hollands, who like Higginson were puzzled by her poems, she said,

"Perhaps you laugh at me! Perhaps the whole United States are laughing at me too! I can't stop for that! My business is to love. I found a bird this morning, down-down on a little bush at the foot of the garden, and wherefore sing, I said, since nobody *hears?*"

Late in 1862, with the war going badly for the North, the Rev. Higginson, now almost forty, resigned his ministry and was appointed colonel of the first regiment of ex-slaves, the First South Carolina Volunteers.

Wounded in battle, Colonel Higginson was mustered out and with his wife went to live in Newport, Rhode Island. In 1870 his book, *Army Life in a Black Regiment*, was published. It is a classic of Civil War literature and history.

While serving with his regiment of newly freed slaves from the Sea Islands off South Carolina, Higginson collected the spirituals he heard them sing. Soon after the war, he published a pioneering article on "Negro Spirituals" in the *Atlantic Monthly*. He was one of the earliest to take significant notice of black culture.

He would never forget that unpublished poet. They would meet one day in Amherst . . .

12

I Find Ecstasy in Living

IN THE FALL OF 1863 Emily began to suffer from a disabling condition of the eyes. It was an aching pain, often severe, coming and going, making it hard to write and even to sleep.

By April 1864 her eyes hurt so badly that she traveled to Boston to seek help from Dr. Henry W. Williams, an eye specialist. The treatment was long and drawn out; she stayed for seven months in nearby Cambridgeport with her beloved cousins, Louisa and Frances Norcross, then twenty-two and seventeen. They were the daughters of Emily's Aunt Lavinia, who had died not long before. She was not allowed to read—the only denial, she said, that made her "trouble." She returned to Boston for treatment from April to October in 1865, staying again with her cousins.

Dr. Williams left no record of his diagnosis. The nature of Emily's eye trouble has never been firmly determined. Some doctors think it was an early symptom of Bright's disease (as her final illness was diagnosed). Others suggest strabismus, glaucoma, or even a psychosomatic condition.

Apart from her earlier visits to Washington and Philadelphia, this was the only other time Emily experienced city life. She joined the Norcross girls in their boardinghouse, just a block from the central business district. She made no effort to sample urban activities, nesting indoors for the most part.

In letters to family or friends, she said living in a city was like living in prison, or "like 8 months in Siberia." Her handwriting in pencil was poor because her vision was so bad. The doctor wouldn't let her go home, so "I work in my Prison, and made Guests for myself." She missed her dog Carlo and the hills at home.

The dating that scholars have assigned her poems indicates she continued to write while in Cambridgeport. Only a few poems reflect her time of treatment. She couldn't see well, but she could hear! Especially when Louisa and Frances recited passages from Shakespeare. Louisa had been lucky enough to hear Fanny Kemble, come to Boston, give readings from the plays. And now the sisters enjoyed reciting from them to entertain Emily. It led Emily, when she got back home, to fly to her bookshelves and devour those luscious passages. "I read them in the garret," she said, "and the rafters wept . . . Why clasp any hand but this, give me ever to drink of this wine."

Her affection for the sisters she called her "little children" was deep, always expressed in a correspondence that ran from 1859 to shortly before her death. Enclosed in those letters were at least twenty-five poems. It was to the Norcross sisters that she revealed how intensely moved she was by the death of Frazar Stearns.

Some scholars studying Emily's life have seen her as the Woman in White refusing to wear any other color, suggesting the whiteness as a symbol of her hermetic life, of her nunlike

Boston in the 1860s held many attractions, but not for Emily Dickinson, who yearned only to return to the familiarity of Amherst.

isolation. But in a letter to the Norcross sisters she teases them about the color in a new cape they had made for her:

> You seem to take a smiling view of my finery. If you know how solemn it was to me, you might be induced to curtail your jests. My sphere is doubtless calicoes, nevertheless I thought it meet to sport a little wool. The mirth it has occasioned will deter me from further exhibition! Won't you tell "the public" that at present I wear a brown dress with a cape if possible browner, and carry a parasol of the same?

The one article of her clothing that survives is a simple white cotton dress, the type worn around the house. Made of patterned dimity, it is quite ordinary, nothing like the fashionable dress of her day.

This is the only surviving example of the exclusively white dresses Dickinson is known to have worn after the mid-1860s. Because of her reticence, dressmakers fitted the poet's garments to her sister, Lavinia Dickinson, who was about the same size.

It was during her second period of treatment in Boston that the Civil War came to an end. In the first months of 1865 the Confederacy fell apart. On April 9, General Lee surrendered to General Grant. The war was over. Five days later, President Lincoln was assassinated while seeing a play at Ford's Theater in Washington.

The fight to end slavery inspired in African Americans the hope that they would find a secure and equal place in American life. But though the experience of black military service, emancipation, and the pressure of black and white abolitionists bent racial discrimination, they did not break it. It would persist long past Emily Dickinson's life.

But search through her letters and you will find no mention of the great events: the reelection of Lincoln; the ending of the war; the murder of the president; the passage of the constitutional amendments establishing freedom, equal citizenship, and the right to vote for African Americans.

What comes up in her poems again and again and again is Death itself. Every day in that Civil War men died. From the newspapers, from the bereaved families, in letters from the front, she heard of death. People lived intimately with it. And in her poems there is no blinking of it. And "the frail Dickinson," wrote the critic Alfred Kazin, "gives us a sudden sense of the most that we can know."

Colonel Higginson, a friend in the thick of events, was never far from her thoughts. In late January 1866 she wrote him a brief note (enclosing a poem) telling him that Carlo had just died. She closed with "Would you instruct me now?" They had not been in touch for some eighteen months.

He wrote back asking her to come visit him while he would be in Boston to lecture. No, she replied, for Father "likes me to travel with him, but objects that I visit." Would he care to come to Amherst instead? "You would find a minute Host but a spacious Welcome." More such exchanges (with more poems sent) took place over the next few years. In one letter Higginson said, "I never relax my interest in what you send to me . . . I think if I could see you once & know that you are real, I might fare better." He wondered how she could live so alone and have "such luminous flashes as come to you."

Meanwhile, in these closing years of the 1860s, the great burst of her creativity that had opened the decade slowed down. She continued to write poems but was never again so prolific. Her themes, her subjects did not change, there was only less expression of them.

And fewer visits to the family next door. The ties between Emily and Sue had frayed for a time. Years would pass without her entering the Evergreens.

In 1870 when the census taker came around, Emily was listed as "Without Occupation." Why not a "Poet"? Webster's Dictionary says an occupation is "the principal business of one's life." And so it was for Emily, as she put it in this poem:

I dwell in Possibility—
A fairer House than Prose—
More numerous of Windows—
Superior—for Doors—
Of Chambers as the Cedars—
Impregnable of Eye—
And for an Everlasting Roof
The Gambrels of the Sky—
Of visitors—the fairest—
For Occupation—This—
The spreading of my narrow Hands
To gather Paradise—

At last, in 1870, Higginson and Emily met face-to-face. He came twice to see her—on the afternoon and the evening of August 16. Late that night he described those two sessions in a letter to his wife. Emily had met him in the entry "with two day lilies which she put in a sort of childlike way into my hand and said 'these are my introduction' in a soft frightened breathless childlike voice." He saw "a little plain woman with two smooth bands of reddish hair . . . in a very plain and exquisitely clean white pique & blue net worsted shawl." She asked him to "forgive me if I am frightened; I never see strangers & hardly know what I say."

She talked "continuously" and "deferentially—sometimes stopping to ask me to talk instead of her—but readily recommencing." He thought she was "thoroughly ingenuous & simple."

Much of what she said was "wise," he told his wife. The last thing she said was "Gratitude is the only secret that cannot reveal itself." And as he left she gave him a photograph of Elizabeth Barrett Browning's grave. He met her father, too, then sixty-seven. Edward Dickinson seemed to Higginson to be "thin dry & speechless . . . not severe I should think but remote."

Thinking about his meeting, he said, "I never was with anyone who drained my nerve power so much. Without touching her, she drew from me. I am glad not to live near her." Many years later, recalling their meeting, he said, "The impression undoubtedly made on me was that of an excess of tension, and of something abnormal."

Unable to forget some of the things Emily said to him in her special way, the next day he jotted them down:

If I read a book and it makes my whole body so cold no fire can ever warm me, I know that is poetry. If I feel physically as if the top of my head were taken off, I know that is poetry. These are the only way I know it. There is no other way. How do most people live without any thoughts . . . How do they get enough strength to put on their clothes in the morning? When I lost the use of my eyes it was a comfort to think there were so few real books that I could easily find someone to read me all of them. Truth is such a rare thing, it is delightful to tell it. I find ecstasy in living—the merest sense of living is joy enough.

Higginson said he asked her if she never felt want of employment, never going off the place and never seeing any visitor. And she replied, "I never thought of conceiving I could ever have the slightest approach to such a want in all future time."

Higginson's impressions are especially noteworthy, for here was a brilliant and sensitive man who knew so many of the leading figures in the literary world, and he recorded how he saw Emily on that very same rare day.

Three years after his first visit, Higginson came again to Amherst to give a lecture, and met Emily. This time he noted only one thing she said: "There is always one thing to be grateful for—that one is one's self & not somebody else."

But Higginson's is not the only impression we have. There is Joseph Lyman's too. He had known Emily since their childhood together and had often talked with her. Later he became a writer for *The New York Times*. In a pen portrait he did of her when they were both in their thirties, he spoke of her eyes as

wondering wells of expression . . . that glance swiftly to the core of all things—hands small, firm, but deft and utterly emancipated from all claspings of perishable things, very firm strong little hands absolutely under control of the brain . . . mouth made for nothing and used for nothing but uttering choice speech, rare thoughts, glittering, starry misty figures, winged words.

13

You Are a Great Poet

AS THE 1870S CAME ON, Emily began to lose family and friends. In 1872 her old playmate Joseph Lyman died of smallpox. Two years later, her father died of a stroke while in Boston on business. After he was buried, Emily was reported to have roamed through the house crying, "Where is he? Emily will find him."

He died without leaving a will, which in effect left the care of his widow and daughters to Austin. There were ample funds for that purpose. Through his law practice and his investments in real estate he had steadily increased his income. His heritage to the town was ample too. Not only had he been crucial to the development of Amherst College, but had recently helped to establish the Massachusetts Agricultural College, today the University of Massachusetts in Amherst.

Recognizing that his affection for his children was held tight and voiceless within, Emily mourned "Father's lonely Life and his lonelier Death." For years she would often dream about him, and waking, wonder where he was. His was a life devoted to the common good, yet lived and died in loneliness.

Tribute to Mr. Dickinson was paid in the obituary in the *Springfield Republican,* almost certainly written by Samuel Bowles. It praised him for having "in these days of cowardly conformity . . . the courage of his convictions."

Only a year after her father died, Emily's mother suffered a stroke, with partial paralysis of hand and foot. With her memory failing too, she asked constantly for her husband, wondering why he didn't come. Emily, writing Higginson about her mother, added that "Home is so far from Home, since my Father died."

And writing to the Norcross sisters, she said, "The birds that Father rescued are trifling in his trees. How flippant are the saved! They were even frolicking at his grave when Vinnie went there yesterday. Nature must be too young to feel, or many years too old."

That summer of 1875, Susan's third child, Thomas Gilbert Dickinson, was born. Everyone would call him Gib.

In her seven remaining years, Emily's mother needed constant attention and of course her daughters had to bear the full responsibility of the household. Mrs. Dickinson died on November 14, 1882. Emily knew her mother, like her father, had not really understood her. Yet, to her Norcross cousins she wrote,

We were never intimate Mother and Children while she was our Mother—but Mines in the same Ground meet by tunneling and when she became our Child, the Affection came—When we were children and she journeyed, she always brought us something. Now would she but bring us herself, what an only Gift . . . She

Girlhood playmate Helen Hunt Jackson(nee Fiske) reentered Dickinson's life after learning of her poetry from Higginson. She strongly but unsuccessfully urged the poet to share her gifts with the world.

slipped from our fingers like a flake gathered by the wind, and is now part of the drift called "the infinite."

Sewall believes that "the greatest tribute that Emily paid her mother lay perhaps in the fact that she never wanted to leave the home that Mrs. Dickinson helped create."

Thanks to Higginson, Emily renewed a connection to a woman she had known during childhood. Helen Hunt was the daughter of an Amherst College professor. The two girls, of the same age but very different in personality, had not been close friends. Helen was an impetuous tomboy who loved to fight. When tuberculosis killed both her parents, she left Amherst, with relatives taking over her care. At twenty-two she married an army engineer, only to suffer appalling losses. Her two young sons died early, and her husband was killed in an accident.

She moved to Newport, Rhode Island, where she met Higginson, living in the same boardinghouse. To support herself she began to write. Higginson guided her, and soon both her poems and prose were appearing in many of the popular magazines. She used her initials, H. H., as her pen name.

Plagued by chronic sore throat, she thought Colorado's better climate might help. There she married William Jackson, a wealthy banker. In the West, she saw firsthand the terrible fate of the Indians. And no longer needing to write for money, she gave herself over to using her talent on their behalf. After long and intensive research, she wrote *A Century of Dishonor* (1881), a bitter indictment of the federal government's betrayal of treaties made with the Indians.

Three years later, determined to reach an even wider audience with her crusade, she wrote a novel, *Ramona*. She hoped it would help the cause of the Indians in the same way Harriet Beecher Stowe's *Uncle Tom's Cabin* had helped the cause of the slaves.

The novel, more romantic than realistic, went through many editions and reached millions more through the movies made of it.

It seems that when Higginson and Helen Hunt were fellow boarders, he showed her some of the poems Emily had sent him, letting her copy them. He wrote Emily that he had met "a lady who once knew you." She and Helen began corresponding, and met in 1873 when Helen stayed briefly in Amherst.

Showing no trace of envy or rivalry, Helen in 1876 wrote Emily that she read her poems "very often—You are a great poet—and it is a wrong to the day you live, that you will not sing aloud. When you are what men call dead, you will be sorry that you were so stingy."

Helen did not give up on breaking through Emily's wall of silence. She kept pressing her to allow her poems to reach the public. And finally, in 1878, she succeeded. Late that year *A Masque of Poets* appeared, published by Roberts Brothers in Boston. Among the many poems was this one of Emily's, unsigned:

Success is counted sweetest
By those who ne'er succeed.
To comprehend a nectar
Requires sorest need.

Not one of all the purple Host
Who took the Flag today
Can tell the definition
So clear of Victory

As he defeated—dying—
On whose forbidden ear
The distant strains of triumph
Burst agonized and clear!

14

O My Too Beloved

HELEN HUNT JACKSON WAS NOT the only one to urge Emily to get out into the world. There were others, though few. One of these was Otis Phillips Lord. Born in 1812, he was more of her father's generation than hers. And like Edward Dickinson, his views placed him in the conservative Whig party. As the Civil War began, he wanted to see the rebels defeated, but believed they had the constitutional right to own slaves. He had moved from leader of the state legislature to a seat on the Massachusetts Supreme Court.

Lord was a gifted talker, both as a public orator and in personal relationships. As a lifelong friend of Emily's father, he and his wife had often been overnight guests at the Dickinsons'. Emily had known him from childhood. After Mrs. Lord died in 1877, the judge and Emily began writing each other almost weekly. His letters were destroyed after Emily's death, but her drafts of letters to him survive.

Judge Otis Lord's death in 1884 was a severe blow to Emily Dickinson.

At this remote distance in time it is hard to see why Emily was attracted to him. Their personalities were so opposite. Sue described the judge as "a perfect figure-head for the Supreme Court, from his stiff stock to his toes . . . His individuality was so bristling, his conviction that he alone was the embodiment of the law, as given on Sinai so entire, his suspicion of all but himself, so deeply founded in the bedrock of old conservative Whig tenacities, not to say obstinacies."

Sewall thinks Emily may have felt a romantic love for Lord just as she had for Bowles: "What she seems to have cherished chiefly in both of them was their vitality, their range of responsiveness, and their extraordinary intellectual vigor."

By 1878 that she was in love with him, and he with her, is clear in her letters. She would write, "O my too beloved. My Darling . . . My Sweet one." Whether he read her poetry, or admired it, no one knows. Although she sent many poems to Higginson, Bowles, and others, perhaps only two fragments of a poem were sent to Lord.

In May 1882, while presiding at a trial, Judge Lord fell so ill that the press reported he might not survive. Emily was terrified at the news. But to her immense relief he recovered.

Scholars think that these lines from a poem of about the same period indicate her intense desire for her lover to come:

I thought the Train would never come—
How slow the whistle sang—
I don't believe a peevish Bird
So whimpered for the Spring—
I taught my Heart a hundred times
Precisely what to say—
Provoking Lover, when you came
Its Treatise flew away

A Fiery Fourth

Early in the morning of July 4, 1879, a fire broke out in Amherst and destroyed the business center. Emily's description of it in a letter to her Norcross cousins is one of the best examples of her sensitivity to details, to color and light and sound:

Dear Cousins,

Did you know there had been a fire here, and that but for a whim of the wind Austin and Vinnie and Emily would have all been homeless? But perhaps you saw the *Republican*.

We were waked by the ticking of the bells,—the bells tick in Amherst for a fire, to tell the firemen.

I sprang to the window, and each side of the curtain saw that awful sun. The moon was shining high at the time, and the birds singing like trumpets.

Emily's description adds epic dimensions to the Amherst fire of 1879.

Vinnie came soft as a moccasin, "Don't be afraid, Emily, it is only the fourth of July."

I did not tell that I saw it, for I thought if she felt it best to deceive, it must be that it was.

She took hold of my hand and led me into mother's room. Mother had not waked, and Maggie was sitting by her. Vinnie left us a moment, and I whispered to Maggie, and asked her what it was.

"Only Stebbins's barn, Emily;" but I knew that the right and left of the village was on the arm of Stebbins's barn. I could hear buildings falling, and oil exploding, and people walking and talking gayly, and cannon soft as velvet from parishes that did not know that we were burning up.

And so much lighter than day was it, that I saw a caterpillar measure a leaf far down in the orchard; and Vinnie kept saying bravely, "It's only the fourth of July."

It seemed like a theatre, or a night in London, or perhaps like chaos. The innocent dew falling "as if it thought no evil," . . . and sweet frogs prattling in the pools as if there were no earth.

At seven people came to tell us that the fire was stopped, stopped by throwing sound houses in as one fills a well.

Mother never waked, and we were all grateful; we knew she would never buy needle and thread at Mr. Cutler's store, and if it were Pompeii nobody could tell her.

The post-office is in the old meeting-house where Loo and I went early to avoid the crowd, and—fell asleep with the bumble-bees and the Lord God of Elijah.

Vinnie's "only the fourth of July" I shall always remember. I think she will tell us so when we die, to keep us from being afraid.

Footlights cannot improve the grave, only immortality.

Forgive me the personality; but I knew, I thought, our peril was yours.

After Emily's mother died in 1882, Lord appears to have proposed marriage. Though she loved him, she could not commit herself. How could she give up her privacy for married life with a public figure? They wrote often, they met often, they embraced, but nothing more. Lord died of a stroke on March 13, 1884. He was seventy-two. She grieved, but she went on.

When Emily lost Lord, it was one terrible blow on top of another. For only six months before, her beloved little nephew and playmate, Gib Dickinson, the eight-year-old son of Sue and Austin, had died a few days after coming down with typhoid fever. To an old family friend, Emily wrote of Gib's last words:

> "Open the Door, open the Door, they are waiting for me," was Gilbert's sweet command in delirium. *Who* were waiting for him, all we possess as we would give to know—Anguish at last opened it, and he ran to the little Grave at his Grandparent's feet—All this and more. Though *is* there more? More than Love and Death? Then tell me its name!

Almost shattered by her youngest child's death, Sue secluded herself for more than a year, never leaving home. For Gib's father the loss of this child was almost too much for him to bear. Neither he nor Emily ever got over the boy's death. "The dyings have been too deep for me," she said, "and before I could raise my heart from one, another has come."

Emily's affection for children was brought out in a memoir of her written after her death by MacGregor Jenkins, one of the neighborhood children allowed onto the Dickinson property. While they were playing games beneath Emily's window it would open and a basket would begin a slow descent on a rope. In it were the gingerbread cakes she liked to bake. He recalled that she supported whatever the kids needed or wanted. "Emily will see that you are supplied (raiding the pantry for cookies or dough-nuts). Emily will see that you are not blamed."

She was always Miss Emily to the children. It was a privilege, they felt, to be asked to give a hand with her chores—watering plants, assisting in the kitchen, running errands.

15

They'll Have to Remember Me

"Another has come . . ."

It all began on June 14, 1884. She was baking a cake when she felt "a great darkness coming" and passed out. Late that night she recovered consciousness, to find Austin and Vinnie and a doctor bending over her. She remained ill for some time. "Nervous strain" they said at first. But then exhaustion, fainting spells, and edema led to the diagnosis of Bright's disease. Today it's called nephritis. It is an inflammation of the kidneys. It can be caused by an infection, or by an immune reaction that goes wrong and injures the kidneys.

More recently, it is thought that kidney trouble was not the cause of her illness. Rather, it might have been severe primary hypertension, or high blood pressure, a diagnosis unknown in her time. Her frequent fainting spells and her final stroke suggest that.

Whatever the case, the remedies given her were of no use. Medicine had a long way to go to come up with effective treatment. Nearly two years would pass before she died. Still, though weakened and grieving over the recent loss of family and friends, she never complained. Her voice in the poems she continued to write—few as these were—doesn't show alarm or fear. It was the voice heard in the letters and poems of the decades before.

From mid-November till early April of the next year acute weakness kept her in bed. Feeling better, she said it felt like the flowering of the arbutus in early spring. She began "to roam in my room a little, an hour at a time."

It was a false hope of recovery. At about ten on the morning of May 13, 1886, she became unconscious. Her doctor said she had suffered a stroke. She remained unconscious, breathing heavily, and on Saturday, May 15, with Austin and Vinnie close by, she died. She was fifty-five years old, still young looking, her reddish bronze hair without a silver thread.

Throughout Emily's final illness, Sue was always on hand to help care for her. It was Sue who prepared the body for burial. She placed flowers at the throat and covered the white casket with them. The grave was lined with the boughs of trees.

The funeral was held in the family library. It was simple and brief. She was buried in the West Cemetery, next to her parents. Flowers bloomed everywhere on that spring day. Her last note, sent to her Norcross cousins, said only, "Called back." These are the words on her tombstone.

A woman who knew the family remembered that when young, Emily had said, "I have a horror of death; the dead are so soon forgotten. But when I die, they'll have to remember me."

In a poem written probably a few months after falling sick, she imagines what might happen:

Dickinson's original gravestone, in the Amherst graveyard just walking distance from her home, just bore the simple initials, E.E.D. But it was later replaced with a more elaborate stone with the message Called Back.

The going from a world we know
To one a wonder still
Is like the child's adversity
Whose vista is a hill,
Behind the hill is sorcery
And everything unknown,
But will the secret compensate
For climbing it alone?

Because I Could Not Stop for Death

Because I could not stop for Death—
He kindly stopped for me—
The Carriage held but just Ourselves—
And Immortality.

We slowly drove—He knew no haste
And I had put away
My labor and my leisure too,
For His Civility—

We passed the School, where Children strove
At Recess—in the Ring—
We passed the Fields of Gazing Grain—
We passed the Setting Sun—

Or rather—He passed Us—
The Dews drew quivering and chill—
For only Gossamer, my Gown—
My Tippet—only Tulle—
We paused before a House that seemed
A swelling of the Ground—
The Roof was scarcely visible—
The Cornice—in the Ground—

Since then—'tis Centuries—and yet
Feels shorter than the Day
I first surmised the Horses' Heads
Were toward Eternity—

Within hours after Emily's passing, Sue wrote a deeply felt obituary for her beloved friend. It was published in the *Springfield Republican*. In it were these passages:

> Her talk and her writings were like no one's else, and although she never published a line, now and then some enthusiastic literary friend would turn love to larceny, and cause a few verses surreptitiously obtained to be printed. Thus, and through other natural ways, many saw and admired her verses, and in consequence frequently notable persons paid her visits, hoping to overcome the protest of her own nature and gain a promise of occasional contributions, at least, to various magazines . . .
>
> Her wagon was hitched to a star—and who could ride or write with such a voyager? A Damascus blade gleaming and glancing in the sun was her wit. Her swift poetic rapture was like the long glistening note of a bird one hears in the June woods at high noon, but can never see. Like a magician she caught the shadowy apparitions of her brain and tossed them in startling picturesqueness to her friends, who, charmed with their simplicity and homeliness as well as profundity, fretted that she had so easily made palpable the tantalizing fancies forever eluding their bungling, fettered grasp. So intimate and passionate was her love of Nature, she seemed herself a part of the high March sky, the summer day and bird-call. Keen and eclectic in her literary tastes, she sifted libraries to Shakespeare and Browning; quick as the electric spark in her intuitions and analyses, she seized the kernel instantly, almost impatient of the fewest words by which she must make her revelation. To her life was rich, and all aglow with God and immortality. With no creed, no formalized faith, hardly knowing the names of dogmas, she walked this life with the gentleness and reverence of

old saints, with the firm step of martyrs who sing while they suffer. How better note the flight of this "soul of fire in a shell of pearl" than by her own words?—

Morns like these, we parted;
Noons like these, she rose;
Fluttering first, then firmer,
To her fair repose.

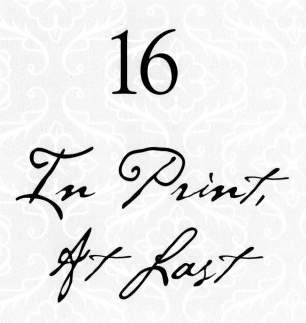

16

In Print, At Last

AFTER EMILY'S DEATH, Vinnie went into her sister's room to sort out her belongings. And in a locked box found some forty notebooks with almost two thousand poems, vastly more than she'd dreamt Emily had written. All were short lyrics, mostly without title. Scholars have traced the publication of some eight poems in the *Springfield Republican*, the *Boston Post*, the *Brooklyn Daily Union*, *Drum Beat*, and *Round Table*. None of the poems carried her name. Eager to have Emily's poems published, Vinnie induced Mabel Loomis Todd, the wife of an Amherst professor, to take on the difficult job of transcribing them from the bits and pieces bound in the fascicles.

It would take years of painstaking labor. Wishing for professional guidance, Mrs. Todd turned to Thomas Wentworth Higginson, the noted author and longtime friend of Emily's, for his advice in choosing the poems they hoped to have published. Higginson doubted if the public would accept the poems in their present form. So he tinkered with them in several ways, to "improve" them by "smoothing out" her unconventional form.

The Boston publisher Roberts Brothers accepted them at once, issuing the volume of 115 *Poems* by Emily Dickinson in 1890. It was an immediate success, running into eleven printings, which led to enlarged editions in 1891 and 1896. With readers wanting to know much more about this magnificent new poet, an edition of her *Letters* appeared in 1894.

The volumes of her poetry were reviewed by the leading magazines. In *Harper's Magazine*, William Dean Howells, the eminent novelist, poet, and editor, said that "if nothing else had come out of our life but this strange poetry we should feel that in the work of Emily Dickinson America, or New England rather, had made a distinctive addition to the literature of the world."

In his essay on Dickinson, the critic Alfred Kazin says that "the years and hours recorded in her work present us with an overwhelming record of one person's most minute reactions to existence . . . one of the fullest records ever left of a *life*, a life whose outlet more and more became poetry."

Source Notes

14 Richard B. Sewall, *The Life of Emily Dickinson* (Cambridge, MA: Harvard University Press, 1980), 37.

15 Ibid., 30.

20 Ibid., 88.

22 Judith Farr, *Emily Dickinson: A Collection of Critical Essays* (Upper Saddle River, NJ: Prentice Hall, 1966) 76, n3.

22 Sewall, 4.

23 Thomas H. Johnson. *The Complete Poems of Emily Dickinson* (Cambridge, MA: Harvard University Press, 1980), 4.

24 Farr, 206.

28 Sewall, 349, n8.

29 Ibid., 342

30 Ibid., 349, n9.

30 Johnson, 640.

31 Sewall, 351.

31 Ibid., 354.

35 Thomas H. Johnson, *Emily Dickinson: Selected Letters* (Cambridge, MA: Belknap Harvard University Press, 1986), 18-19.

36 Ibid., 19-20

37 Farr, 222.

39 Cynthia Griffin Wolff, *Emily Dickinson* (Reading, PA: Perseus Books, 1988), 155, n8.

39 Sewall, 686.

40 Farr, 222.

40 Sewall, 360.

40 Ibid., 361.

43 Paula Bennett, *Emily Dickinson: Woman Poet* (Iowa City: University of Iowa Press, 1959), 7.

43 Alfred Habegger, *My Wars are Laid Away in Books: The Life of Emily Dickinson* (New York: Modern Library, 2002), 235, n5.

43 Ibid, 235, n4.

44 Bennett, 4.

44 Habegger, 217.

44 Johnson (*Poems*), 658.

44 Habegger, 225.

45 Sewall, 420

45 Ibid., 91.

49 Johnson (*Poems*), 286.

50 Sewall, 101.

52 Ibid., 145

53 Johnson (*Letters*), 16.

54 Sewall, 416.

54 Ibid., 418-419.

55 Ibid., 396

55 Ibid.

55 Johnson (*Poems*), 277.

59 Herbert G. Gutman, *Who Built America* (New York: Pantheon, 1989) Vol I, 404.

60 Sewall, 445

60 Ibid., 446

60 Ibid., 444

61 Ibid., 446

62 Ibid., 452.

62 Ibid., 454

62 Habegger, 334.

67 Ibid., 388

70 Johnson (*Poems*), 634.

70 Judith Farr, *The Passion of Emily Dickinson* (Cambridge, MA: Harvard University Press, 2000), 350, n13.

75 Sewall, 87, n9.

76 Ibid., 468.

77 Habegger, 375.

81 Johnson (*Poems*), 350-351.

84 Ibid., 145

84 Farr (*Essays*), 53

86 Johnson (*Letters*) 173.

86 Ibid., 166.

86 Ibid., 175.

87 Ibid., 176.

87 Ibid., 177.

89 Habegger, 490.

90 Sewall, 629.

92 Alfred Kazin, *An American Procession* (New York: Knopf, 1987), 180.

93 Johnson (*Poems*), 198.

93 Ibid., 327.

95 Johnson (*Letters*), 207-211.

95 Sewall, 566.

95 Ibid., 425.

97 Habegger, 562.

97 Johnson (*Letters*), 230.

97 Ibid.

98 Sewall, 89.

99 Ibid., 580

100 Johnson (*Poems*), 35.

103 Sewall, 248.

103 Ibid., 661, n8.

103 Johnson (*Poems*), 615

105 Sewall, 144.

106 Susan Howe, *My Emily Dickinson* (Berkeley, CA: North Atlantic Books, 1985), 134.

106 Sewall, 125.

107 Habegger, 547.

109 Farr (*Passion*), 373, n6.

110 Johnson (*Poems*), 662.

111 Ibid., 350.

113 Ellen Louise Hart and Martha Nell Smith, *Open Me Carefully: Emily Dickinson's Intimate Letters to Susan Huntington Dickinson* (Ashfield, MA: Paris Press, 1998) 266-268.

114 Ibid., 65.

115 Habegger, 628.

115 Kazin, 166.

Selected Bibliography

Why "selected"? Because the biographical and critical literature on Emily Dickinson is vast, and increases almost every year. A great many editions of the poems themselves have appeared since the first was published in 1890. And the number of scholarly studies of one aspect or another of her life and work multiplies. I list chiefly those I have used. A fuller bibliography may be found in *The Cambridge Companion to Emily Dickinson*.

POEMS AND LETTERS

Johnson, Thomas H., ed. *The Complete Poems of Emily Dickinson*. Boston: Little Brown, 1960.

Johnson, Thomas H., and Theodora Ward, eds. *The Letters of Emily Dickinson*, 3 vols. Cambridge, MA: The Belknap Press of Harvard University Press, 1958.

WORKS ABOUT EMILY DICKINSON

Bennett, Paula. *Emily Dickinson: Woman Poet*. Iowa City: University of Iowa Press, 1958.

Eberwine, Jane Donohue, ed. *An Emily Dickinson Encyclopedia*. Westport, CT: Greenwood Press, 1998.

Farr, Judith. *The Passion of Emily Dickinson*. Cambridge, MA: Harvard University Press, 2000.

Farr, Judith, ed. *Emily Dickinson: A Collection of Critical Essays.* Upper Saddle River, NJ: Prentice Hall, 1996.

Habegger, Alfred. *My Wars Are Laid Away in Books: The Life of Emily Dickinson.* New York: Modern Library, 2002.

Hart, Ellen Louise, and Martha Nell Smith, eds. *Open Me Carefully: Emily Dickinson's Intimate Letters to Susan Huntington Dickinson.* Ashfield, MA: Paris Press, 1998.

Howe, Susan. *My Emily Dickinson.* Berkeley, CA: North Atlantic Books, 1985.

Kazin, Alfred. *A Writer's America.* New York: Knopf, 1988.

———. *An American Procession.* New York: Knopf, 1984.

Kelly, Catherine E. *In the New England Fashion: Reshaping Women's Lives in the Nineteenth Century.* Ithaca, NY: Cornell University Press, 1999.

Martin, Wendy, ed. *The Cambridge Companion to Emily Dickinson.* Cambridge, MA: Cambridge University Press, 2002.

Phillips, Kate. *Helen Hunt Jackson: A Literary Life.* Berkeley, CA: University of California Press, 1998.

Sewall, Richard B. *The Life of Emily Dickinson.* Cambridge, MA: Harvard University Press, 1980.

Turco, Lewis, ed. *Emily Dickinson: Woman of Letters.* Albany: State University of New York Press, 1993.

Wolff, Cynthia Griffin. *Emily Dickinson.* Reading, PA: Perseus Books, 1988.

Both Scholastic and Barnes & Noble have published inexpensive paperback editions of the poems, and Dover Publications the collection of her letters that first appeared in 1894.

Plays, films, videos, and audio recordings have been produced on various aspects of Dickinson's life and works. Many composers have created musical settings of her poems.

Chronology of Emily Dickinson's Life

1775   Samuel Fowler Dickinson, grandfather, born.

1803   Edward Dickinson, father, born.

1804   Emily Norcross, mother, born.

1828   Edward and Emily Norcross marry.

1829   Their son, Austin, born.

1830   Emily, daughter, born on December 10.

1833   Lavinia (Vinnie), Emily's sister, born.

1835   Emily begins four years at primary school.

1840   Emily enters Amherst Academy.

1847   Emily boards at Mount Holyoke Female Seminary.

1848   Parents withdraw her from Mount Holyoke because of delicate health.

1850   Emily's valentine poem published in Amherst College paper.

1851   Emily and Vinnie taken to Boston to see lung specialist.

1852   A Dickinson poem appears in *Springfield Republican*. Father elected to Congress.

1853   Amherst–Belchertown Railroad opens.

1855	Emily and Vinnie visit Washington and Philadelphia. The Dickinsons move to the Homestead on Main Street, Emily's home until her death.
1856	Austin Dickinson marries Susan Gilbert. They live at the Evergreens, adjoining Emily's home. Samuel Bowles, editor of *Springfield Republican*, becomes family friend.
1857	Ralph Waldo Emerson and Wendell Phillips lecture in Amherst and meet the Dickinsons.
1858	Emily's most prolific period writing poems begins. She assembles her poems in bound packets.
1860	Lincoln elected president. Rev. Charles Wadsworth visits Emily.
1861	Civil War begins. Emily composes over 200 poems. One poem, unsigned, published in *Springfield Republican*. Austin and Sue have first child, Ned.
1862	Another poem in *Springfield Republican*. Emily writes first of several letters to Thomas Wentworth Higginson, asking for literary advice.
1864	Emily to Boston for eye treatment, staying seven months. Austin drafted to Union army, but pays $500 for substitute.
1865	Emily again to Boston for eye treatment, April to October. Higginson, colonel of black regiment, wounded. Civil War ends.
1866	Helen Hunt Jackson meets Higginson in Newport. Her childhood connection to Emily reestablished. Another Dickinson poem in *Springfield Republican*.
1870	Higginson visits Emily in Amherst.
1873	Helen Hunt Jackson visits Emily, urging her to publish. Judge Otis Phillips Lord and wife visit Dickinsons.

1874	Emily's father dies in Boston.
1875	Mother paralyzed. Emily helps nurse her for next seven years. Austin and Susan's third child, Thomas Gilbert (Gib) Dickinson, born.
1877	Bowles visits Emily. Mrs. Lord dies.
1878	Emily courted by Judge Lord. Despite ardent correspondence, she refuses to marry. First poem by Emily to appear in a book, *A Masque of Poets.*
1881	Mabel Loomis Todd and her husband, professor of astronomy at Amherst College, enter Dickinson circle.
1882	Emily's mother dies. Charles Wadsworth dies.
1883	Gib Dickinson at dies age eight.
1884	Judge Lord dies. Emily has first attack of final illness.
1885	Emily bedridden with illness.
1886	Emily dies on May 15, and is buried in West Cemetery, Amherst, beside her parents.
1890	*Poems* by Emily Dickinson, eds. Mabel Loomis Todd and T. W. Higginson, published by Roberts Brothers, Boston.
1891	*Poems*, second series, eds. Higginson and Todd, published.
1894	*Letters of Emily Dickinson*, 2 vols., ed. Mabel Loomis Todd, published.

Austin died in 1895, Vinnie in 1899, Susan in 1913, and Mabel Todd in 1932.

Visiting the Emily Dickinson Sites

The Dickinson Homestead, the poet's birthplace, and her home for the greater part of her life, and the Evergreens, next door, where her brother, Austin, and his family lived, are open to the public for tours from March through mid-December. The Homestead is at 280 Main Street, Amherst, Massachusetts, and the Evergreens at 214 Main Street. The Homestead can be reached by phoning (413) 542-8161 or by e-mailing Info@dickinson-home stead.org.

The Jones Library, Special Collections, offers exhibits devoted to Dickinson. For those who wish to keep abreast of new material on Dickinson there are *The Emily Dickinson Journal, Dickinson Studies,* and *The Bulletin of the Emily Dickinson International Society.*

Index

Page numbers in *italics* refer to illustrations.

Abolitionism, 25, *25*, 80, 82
Aids to English Composition (Parker), 29–30
Amherst, Lord Jeffrey, 12
Amherst Academy, 13, 16, 26–31, *28*, 40
Amherst College, 13–14, 27, 53, 58, 96
Amherst fire of 1879, *104*, 104–105
*Appeal in Favor of That Class of Americans
    Called Africans, An* (Child), 25
Army Life in a Black Regiment (Higginson), 87
Atlantic Monthly, 20, 82, 87

"Because I Could Not Stop For Death"
    (Dickinson), 111
Bennett, Paul, 43
Bible, the, 27, *38*, 39, 76
Black Cake recipe, 74–75, *75*
Boston, Massachusetts, 88, 89, *90*
Boston Post, 114
Bowles, Mary, 66, 67
Bowles, Samuel, 65–67, *66*, 69, 76, 82, 97
Bright's disease, 89, 108
Brontë, Charlotte, 38, 44, 67
Brontë, Emily, 38, 67
Brooklyn Daily Union, 114
Brown, John, 78
Browning, Elizabeth Barrett, 39, 67, 69,
    81–82, 94
Burns, Anthony, 82–83

Caesar, Julius, 27
Carlo (dog), 44–45, 89, 92
Century of Dishonor, A (Hunt), 99
Cherokee Indians, 25
Child, Lydia Maria, 19
Cicero, 27

Civil War, 79, 80, 87, 92, 101
Coleman, Eliza, 61
Compromise of 1850, 59, 78
Currier, Nathan, 33

Dartmouth College, 15
Depression of 1837, 24
Dickens, Charles, 38
Dickinson, Austin, 14, *26*, 46, 53, 65–67,
    96, 108, 109
    birth of, 17
    Civil War and, 80, 81
    courtship and marriage of, 47, 50
    death of, 119
    death of son and, 106
    Emily, relationship with, 45–47
    as lawyer, 46, 62
Dickinson, Edward, *17*, 22, 29, 46, 69, 77,
    92–94, 101
    Amherst College and, 14, 45, 96
    children, relationship with, 24, 56, 76,
        97
    courtship and marriage of, 16–17
    death of, 96
    education of, 16
    homes of, 18, 21, 62
    as lawyer, 12, 16, 20, 96
    political career of, 58–60, 62, 80
    railroads and, 48–49
    religion and, 39
Dickinson, Edward (Ned), 81
Dickinson, Emily, *26*
    Bible and, 38, 39
    birth of, 11, 15, 18
    Bowles, relationship with, 65–67, 69

brother (Austin), relationship with, 45–47
childhood of, 18, 21–23
children, affection for, 106–107
clothing of, 89–91, *91*, 94
dating of poems, 84, 89
death in poems of, 92
death of, 109
domestic work and, 18–19, 36, 64, 72
education of, 20, 22–24, 26–37, 40
family of, 11–18
fascicles of poems by, 77–78
father (Edward), relationship with, 24, 56, 76, 96–97
favorite authors of, 38–39, 44
gardening and, 20, 31
gravestone of, 109, *110*
health of, 40, 57, 88–89, 108–109
Higginson, relationship with, 82–87, 92–95, 98, 103
homes of, *13*, 15, *18*, 18, 21, *22*, 62, *63*
isolation of, 22, 65, 89
letters of, 35, 36, 38, 45, 60, 67, 71–72, *73*, *83*, 89, 104–105
Lord, relationship with, 101, 103, 106
mother (Emily Norcross), relationship with, 63–64, 97–98
music and, 23, 37, 40
obituary for, 112–113
pet of, 44–45, 89, 92
physical appearance of, 29, 70, 86, 94, 95, 109
poetry quoted, 23, 24, 30, 44, 49, 55, 69–70, 81, 84, 93, 100, 103, 110, 111
religion and, 39, 40
sister-in-law (Susan), relationship with, 47, 50, 72, 93, 109, 112–113
sister (Vinnie), relationship with, 50–52
travels of, 60–61, 89
valentines by, 53–54
Wadsworth, relationship with, 61–62
writing style of, 29–30
Dickinson, Emily Norcross, 11, *19*, 23, 29, 96, 105
children, relationship with, 63–64, 97–98
courtship and marriage of, 16–17
death of, 106
domestic skill of, 19–20, 74
health of, 18, 20, 63–64, 72, 97

Dickinson, Lavinia (Vinnie), *26*, 31, *52*, 56, 60, 61, 91, 96, 97, 105, 108, 109
birth of, 18
childhood of, 18–19, 50
death of, 119
domestic work and, 18–19, 64, 72
Emily, relationship with, 50–52
Emily's poems and, 114
Dickinson, Lucretia Gunn, *14*, 15
Dickinson, Samuel Fowler, 12–16, *14*, 18, 21
Dickinson, Susan Gilbert, 45, 46, *47*, 64, 66, 67, 76, 81, 97
courtship and marriage of, 47, 50
death of, 119
death of son and, 106
Emily, relationship with, 47, 50, 72, 93, 109, 112–113
obituary for Emily written by, 112–113
Dickinson, Thomas Gilbert (Gib), 97, 106
Dickinson Homestead, Amherst, *13*, 15, *18*, 18, 21, 62–63, 72
Dred Scott decision (1857), 78
Drum Beat, 114

Eliot, George (Mary Ann Evans), 38–39
Emerson, Ralph Waldo, 38, 44, 50, 76, 78
Emmons, Henry Vaughan, 56, *57*, 57
Evergreens, The, Amherst, 62, *64*, 72, 76, 93

Familiar Lectures in Botany (Phelps), 31
First South Carolina Volunteers, 87
Fiske, Daniel, 29
Franklin, R.W., 84
Freedom's Advocate, 25
French and Indian War, 11, 12
Frugal Housewife, The (Child), 19
Fugitive Slave Law of 1850, 82

Garrison, William Lloyd, *25*
Gilbert, Harriet, 50
Gilbert, Thomas, 50
Graves, John, 56, *57*, 57
Greeley, Horace, 22

Harpers Ferry, Virginia, 78
Harper's Magazine, 20, 115
Harvard College, 27
Hawthorne, Nathaniel, 39
Higginson, Thomas Wentworth, 82–87, *85*, 92–95, 97–99, 114–115

Holland, Sophia, 29, 60
Howells, William Dean, 115
Humphrey, Jane, 55
Humphrey, Leonard, 53
Hunt Jackson, Helen, *98*, 98–101
Hutchinson Family, 37

Jackson, Andrew, 25
Jackson, William, 99
Jacksonian Democrats, 58, 59
Jane Eyre (Brontë), 44
Jenkins, MacGregor, 106–107
Jones, Amelia (Mrs. George L. Stearns), 37
Journal of a Residence on a Georgian Plantation
      (Kemble), 67, 69

Kavanaugh (Longfellow), 39
Kazin, Alfred, 92, 115
Kemble, Fanny, 67, *68*, 69, 89

Letters of Emily Dickinson, 115
"Letter to a Young Contributor"
      (Higginson), 82
Liberator, The, 25
Lincoln, Abraham, 59, 78–79, 92
Lind, Jenny, 37
Longfellow, Henry Wadsworth, 39
Lord, Otis Phillips, 101, *102*, 103
Lyman, Joseph, 95, 96
Lyon, Mary, 33, *34*, 35, 36, 40, 41, 53

Maher, Maggie, 72, 76, 105
Masque of Poets, A, 100
Massachusetts Agricultural College, 96
Melville, Herman, 39
Mexican War, 53
Mount Holyoke Female Seminary, 31–37,
      33, 40–41, 53

Native Americans, 25, 44, 99
Newton, Benjamin F., 44, 56
Norcross, Emily, 40
Norcross, Frances, 88–90, 97
Norcross, Lavinia, 29, 88
Norcross, Louisa, 67, 88–90, 97

O'Brien, Margaret, 72

Phelps, Almira, 31

Phillips, Wendell, 76
Poe, Edgar Allan, 77–78
Poems (Dickinson), 115
Poems (Emerson), 44
Presidential election of 1860, 78–79

Railroads, 48–49
Ramona (Hunt), 99
Republican party, 59, 78–79
Revolutionary War, 11
Roberts Brothers, 100, 115
Root, Abiah, 34
Round Table, 114

"Safe in Alabaster Chambers" (Dickinson),
      73
Seneca Falls Convention of 1848, 41–43
Sewall, Richard B., 20, 31, 40, 55, 98, 103
Shakespeare, William, 38, 76, 89
Slavery, 25, 59, 78, 79, 80, 82–83, 92
Springfield Republican, 54, 65, 69, 97, 114
Stanton, Elizabeth Cady, 42, *42*
Stearns, Frazar, 81
Stowe, Harriet Beecher, 39, 99

Thoreau, Henry David, 38
Todd, Mabel Loomis, 114, 119
Turner, Kate, 77
Turner, Nat, 25
Twain, Mark, 62

Uncle Tom's Cabin (Stowe), 39, 99
Underground Railroad, 82
University of Massachusetts in Amherst, 96

Virgil, 27
"Vision of Poets, A" (Browning), 39
Voting rights, 33

Wadsworth, Charles, *61*, 61–62
Washington, George, 60
Whig party, 58, 59, 101
Whitman, Walt, 39
Wilbur, Richard, 83–84
Williams, Henry W., 88
Women's rights movement, 41, *42*

Yale College, 16, 27

About the Author

The life of Emily Dickinson is the sixth biography of American poets that Milton Meltzer has written for Twenty-First Century Books. He has now published more than one hundred books for young people and adults in the fields of history, biography, and social issues. Most recently his work has included editing anthologies of poetry bearing on aspects of American history.

Two of his many awards include the Laura Ingalls Wilder Award and the Regina Medal, both for lifetime achievement in children's literature. He has also won the Christopher, Jane Addams, Carter G. Woodson, Jefferson Cup, Washington Book Guild, Olive Branch, and Golden Kite awards. Five of his books have been finalists for the National Book Award.

Born in Worcester, Massachusetts, Meltzer was educated at Columbia University. He lives with his wife in New York City. They have two daughters and two grandsons.